THE ULTIMATE GUIDE

THE ULTIMATE GUIDE

BY MICHAEL GOLDMAN

CONTENTS

FOREWORD

Welcome to *24: The Ultimate Guide*!

This book summarizes, elaborates on, and celebrates over six years of extremely hard work by a large group of talented people who first came together several years ago to produce an offbeat concept, at best. That concept—an episodic television program told in real-time over the course of a 24-hour period.

I recall running the idea past my colleague, and the show's co-creator, Robert Cochran and both of us agreed the concept would be difficult to sell to a major network. But thanks to the backing we received from Imagine Entertainment and 20th Century Fox Television, the show not only worked, it surpassed all our expectations.

All of which led to a new problem—how could we possibly document the whole thing for our fans? *24: The Ultimate Guide* addresses that issue.

Thanks to the efforts of writer Michael Goldman and DK Publishing, we've created the most comprehensive, authoritative, and exclusive look ever assembled about the first six years of the expanding "24" universe, and the people, stories, technology, and themes that populate that universe.

It's our hope you enjoy devouring this chronicle of where "24" has been. Now, we just have to figure out where we're going next...

Joel Surnow
24 Co-Creator/Executive Producer

JACK BAUER

Jack Bauer is an elite CTU (Counter-Terrorist Unit) operative with a distinguished, albeit controversial, record of doggedly pursuing terrorists on American soil. Bauer has earned fame for a series of selfless, often reckless, deeds during various classified operations, particularly during what have come to be known as Days 1 through 6—terror plots exposed, prevented, or mitigated all on single days. This way of life has brought tragic personal consequences for Bauer and made him increasingly desperate to escape his line of work, but events spiraling out of control always force him back to the front lines.

JACK BAUER

Jack Bauer, the nation's pre-eminent counter-terrorist field agent, epitomizes the sacrifices and moral quandaries confronting those on the front lines of America's ongoing War on Terror, but he's paid a terrible price for his commitment. Once a by-the-book agent, he has evolved into an operative with a reputation as a loose cannon all too willing to bend or break rules, commit acts of horrifying violence, or even sacrifice lives as he pursues the greater good. These tactics have made him hundreds of enemies, led indirectly to his wife's murder, a strained relationship with his daughter, deadly confrontations with his father and brother, a serious drug addiction, months in a foreign prison, and an inability to maintain healthy personal relationships. Still, those who have worked closely with Bauer, or seen him perform almost mythical deeds to save innocent lives, regard him as a selfless avenging angel, and a necessary last line of defense in an increasingly dark and desperate struggle.

Jack Bauer's "smart card" ID will be scanned into CTU's HID bioCLASS reader system. The device verifies on three levels—smart card reading, inputting PIN via keypad, and a positive finger touchpad scan.

Although, early in his CTU career, Jack Bauer carried a Sig Sauer P226 9mm Luger as his primary field weapon, in recent years, he has preferred the Heckler and Koch (HK) USP Compact 9mm pistol, pictured here.

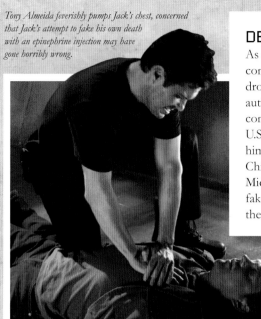

Tony Almeida feverishly pumps Jack's chest, concerned that Jack's attempt to fake his own death with an epinephrine injection may have gone horribly wrong.

DEAD AND GONE

As events surrounding Bauer's Day 4 mission concluded, it became necessary for him to drop out of sight to avoid capture by Chinese authorities for his illegal assault on their consulate, or worse, being killed by shadowy U.S. government forces determined to prevent him from revealing national secrets to the Chinese. With assistance from Tony Almeida, Michelle Dessler, and Chloe O'Brian, Bauer faked his own death and "went dark" for the next 18 months.

RELEASED

The Chinese government eventually caught up with Bauer at the end of Day 5. As the tragic events of Day 6 unfold, he returns to the U.S. after 18 months in a Chinese military prison—filthy, burned, and scarred from torture—as part of a secret deal brokered between President Wayne Palmer and the Chinese government. The Chinese opted not to kill Bauer, instead they attempted to brutally extract valuable intelligence information. Bauer remained silent during his captivity, but there are reports that he was duped into unintentionally exposing an American mole during an escape attempt manipulated by his captors.

FACT FILE

AGE: 41

BIRTHPLACE: Santa Monica, CA

MARITAL STATUS: Widowed

CHILDREN: Daughter, Kimberly Bauer

RELATIVES: Phillip Bauer (father, deceased), Graem Bauer (brother, deceased), Marilyn Bauer (sister-in-law), Josh Bauer (nephew)

EDUCATION:
- Bachelor of Arts, English Literature—UCLA
- Master of Science, Criminology and Law— UC Berkeley
- LAPD – Basic SWAT School
- Special Forces Operations Training Course

GOVERNMENT EXPERIENCE:
- CTU (Los Angeles Domestic Unit)—Former Special Agent in Charge/Field Operations Director/Field Agent
- Department of Defense, Washington DC— Special Assistant to the Secretary of Defense
- LAPD—Special Weapons and Tactics

MILITARY:
- US Army Combat Applications Group
- US Army First Special Forces Operational Detachment
- Team Delta (Delta Force)

FIELD GEAR

Like any agent, the equipment Jack Bauer carries into the field varies wildly depending on the mission and situation on the ground. But under ideal circumstances, Bauer normally brings a canvas messenger bag on missions to carry a variety of weapons and tactical equipment. Among them: his HK USP Compact pistol, bulletproof vest, knife, flashlight, cell phone, PDA, and other devices.

HK USP Compact 9mm pistol in leather paddle holster

Pocket monoscope (sight magnification device), 10x24 magnification up to 288 feet

Jack Bauer's official CTU badge

Second Chance all-Kevlar bulletproof torso vest

Doxa Sharkhunter SUB 750T military diver's watch, depth rating up to 750 meters

CTU standard issue stun gun

Jack Bauer's CTU identification card, with photo, barcode, and encrypted data strip

Benchmade automatic switchblade with half-serrated edge

Mini Tigerlight flashlight

Motorola i880 cell phone. Includes GPS locator chip, walkie-talkie function, camera, satellite download capability, and push-button flip-top

JACK BAUER

Jack Bauer was raised in Santa Monica, California, the eldest of two sons in a German-American family that eventually grew wealthy, thanks to the business built by his father, Phillip Bauer. After college, he chose a military and law enforcement career, distinguishing himself in the US Army's Delta Force, and later briefly joining the Los Angeles Police Department's SWAT division. Eventually, government officials recruited him to join CTU Los Angeles. His decision to pursue this career led to almost a decade of estrangement between Bauer and his father, who had hoped he would take over the family business. Meanwhile, Bauer married graphic designer Teri and had a daughter, Kimberley. Since his wife was murdered six years ago, Bauer has had a strained and difficult relationship with Kimberly, now a 22-year-old woman.

FAMILY PORTRAIT

Jack Bauer with his late wife, Teri (left), then 34, and their daughter, Kimberley, then 15. For many years, Teri was a graphic designer and artist in Los Angeles, working in advertising, at museums, and in the comic book industry. The pressure and danger of Jack's career strained the Bauer marriage at one point, and for a period, Jack moved out and had a brief affair with his CTU colleague, Nina Myers, while Teri had a brief affair of her own with Dr. Phil Parslow.

Nina Myers (right) appears to comfort Teri Bauer shortly after Teri was rescued from Ira Gaines. However, it turned out that Myers was a mole operating under deep cover at CTU, about to betray Jack and murder Teri.

A listless Jack Bauer, still in mourning and holding a picture of his late wife, Teri Bauer, ignores calls summoning him back to CTU early on Day 2. Although he avenged his wife and squared accounts with Nina several years later, Bauer has never fully recovered from Teri's death, and the event continues to affect him to this day.

FACT FILE

NAME: Kimberley Bauer

AGE: 22

BIRTHPLACE: Santa Monica, CA

MARITAL STATUS: Single

RELATIVES: Jack Bauer (father), Teri (mother, deceased), Phillip Bauer (grandfather, deceased), Graem Bauer (uncle, deceased), Marilyn Bauer (aunt), Josh Bauer (cousin)

EDUCATION:
- Santa Monica High School (did not graduate)
- Earned GED Certificate; Santa Monica College
- Associate of Arts in Computer Programming

EXPERIENCE:
- Intern, CTU Los Angeles, Domestic Unit
- Level One Data Analyst, CTU Los Angeles Domestic Unit
- Nanny/childcare positions

Phillip Bauer

RELATIONSHIPS

Jack Bauer's line of work is hardly conducive to successful romantic relationships. His marriage had rocky moments, an affair with Nina Myers proved disastrous, and after Teri's death, he only found temporary solace in the arms of some of the women involved in his adventures, such as Kate Warner. But only Audrey Raines, daughter of former Secretary of Defense James Heller, seems to have made a lasting emotional impact on Jack.

Marilyn, Josh, and Graem Bauer—Jack's sister-in-law, nephew, and brother. Marilyn married Graem after previously dating Jack, and the marriage was unhappy from the start. Graem and Jack's relationship eventually declined, and Graem took over Jack's position as heir to their father's business. Graem later became involved in a shadowy terrorist conspiracy that ultimately led to his demise. Both Marilyn's future, and her feelings for Jack, remain unclear.

Blood Links

Jack Bauer's relationship with his father, Phillip, soured years ago when Jack chose not to join Phillip's business, BXJ Technologies. Phillip then picked Jack's brother, Graem, to head the company. For almost a decade, Jack did not speak to his father, and eventually severed contact with his brother as well. Phillip and Graem steered BXJ into murky legal waters, and eventually helped Russian terrorists obtain Sentox VX Nerve Gas and manipulated President Logan during Day 5. As Day 6 unfolded, Jack found leads that pointed to BXJ's involvement in helping Russian arms dealer Dimitri Gredenko acquire suitcase nuclear bombs. As Jack forced the truth from Graem, Phillip Bauer decided to destroy evidence linking his company to terrorists. That meant, among other things, murdering Graem, setting up Jack to be ambushed, and holding his grandson, Josh Bauer, hostage. Phillip returned near the end of Day 6, determined to kidnap his grandson and take him to China. Josh Bauer shot Phillip, and Jack Bauer then left his father to die in order to save his nephew.

Nina Myers served as Jack's Chief of Staff, which eventually led them into a brief affair during Jack's separation from his wife. Although the affair ended, Jack continued to trust Nina professionally—a fatal mistake.

Bauer met Kate Warner during Day 2 when he saved her from terrorists. That day led to a romantic relationship between the two, but it eventually ended in the years between Day 2 and Day 3.

Bauer romanced Claudia Salazar while undercover in the Salazar drug cartel before Day 3. During Day 3, he attempted to help Claudia escape from Hector Salazar, only to see her tragically killed in the attempt.

Audrey Raines is the first woman since Teri Bauer that Jack has deeply loved. They had an affair before Day 4, but their relationship hit a rocky patch later, during Day 4. Eventually, during Day 5, he admitted he loved her.

Diane Huxley offered solace to Bauer when he was in hiding, working on an oil rig. During Day 5, he saved her son, Derek, from death, but confessed to Diane that he was still in love with Audrey Raines.

The Counter Terrorist Unit (CTU) is an elite branch of the CIA, established after the 1993 World Trade Center bombing as a domestic agency responsible for protecting U.S. targets from terror attacks. CTU is controlled by a District Command system, which oversees a series of Division Command offices that, in turn, operate various domestic units based in most major U.S. cities. At one point during Day 5, the Department of Homeland Security briefly absorbed CTU, but the agency reverted to its previous command structure after that crisis.

CTU BULLPEN

The nerve center of CTU's Los Angeles Domestic Unit is the so-called bullpen—a sophisticated data collection and analysis area located on the ground floor of the CTU building. At their workstations, CTU analysts sift through trillions of gigabytes of data each day, using the world's most sophisticated, networked computer technology, interlinked with major law enforcement databases across the globe plus state and local emergency systems. Senior analysts, like Chloe O'Brian, work at separate, large stations (below), while other analysts are grouped together to allow for more efficient collaboration. Even the smallest details of the bullpen are strategically designed to increase efficiency and collaborative capabilities. For instance, circular overhead halo-style lighting was created to directly illuminate the workstation desks below, and ergonomic Humanscale Freedom chairs were brought in to maximize the comfort and alertness levels of analysts who are at their stations for hours at a time. Information sharing is so central in the facility that, in addition to the networked computer monitors at each station, a series of strategically hung screens constantly exhibit data to the entire room—three 50-inch Panasonic Plasma screens and four 24-inch Dell 2407WFP monitors on the far wall.

The circular area represents the main CTU bullpen, where most CTU data analysts are clustered. Elsewhere on the floor are smaller bullpen stations where 2—3 analysts can be positioned in various configurations.

Display screen on Chloe O'Brian's desk, featuring the standard CTU computer operating system interface, showing satellite surveillance imagery.

Chloe O'Brian's workstation is centrally located to allow her to view the entire bullpen area. Her station features a cornucopia of the latest computer technology, including three 20-inch Macintosh Cinema Display screens connected to a trio of Macintosh 2.3 dual processor G5 desktop towers.

CTU uses Cisco Unified IP 7900-series telephone technology, with eight-line functionality, VoIP (Voice-over Internet Protocol) capabilities, and distinctive ring-tone.

As the highest-ranking agent on site, Special Agent in Charge Bill Buchanan had a private office overlooking the bullpen, which he kept sparse. Like all CTU workstations, Buchanan's office had a networked computer system with a 27-inch Dell (2707WFP) multimedia display. Note the bulletproof windows with frosted striping for privacy. Some CTU agents speculate the stripes represent an actual bar-code message.

CTU CENTRAL

CTU moved into this new building in an undisclosed Los Angeles location some time during the 18 months between Day 3 and Day 4. The facility became more spacious and secure with concrete walls and stairs replacing the metallic infrastructure of the original CTU. This view illustrates probably the busiest zone in the facility during moments of crisis—Chloe O'Brian's workstation on the second floor, directly adjacent to the Situation Room conference area, and directly beneath the third floor office of the Special Agent in Charge which was designed to overlook the entire bullpen area.

Although CTU has a larger, conference room, when a crisis breaks, the Situation Room is preferred due to its secure infrastructure. The room features teleconferencing technology, and a wall-mounted 50-inch Panasonic Plasma display, but it also functions as a safe room during environmental attacks, since it's equipped with metal seal technology. During Day 5, this capability saved several lives during the Sentox nerve gas attack.

CTU FACILITIES

*C*TU Los Angeles is located in a concrete and steel reinforced building that, from the outside, is non-descript, since its exact location is classified. But inside, CTU is a state-of-the-art, ultra-secure, "smart building" built to maximize efficiency, provide logistical support for field teams, and offer instant analysis on unfolding terror scenarios. CTU is equipped with a heliport, medical clinic, interrogation and observation rooms, holding rooms, and tech rooms where delicate computer equipment operates around the clock. The facility also has multiple conference rooms, the analysts' bullpen, an executive office, and fully operational offices for visiting officials from District, Division, the CIA, DoD, and other agencies. CTU is also wired with the latest audio-visual technology, and ultra-fast fiber-optic and satellite communications gear.

FIRST FLOOR

The first floor of the current CTU Los Angeles building is far more spacious than the original building—CTU moved into new quarters between Day 3 and Day 4. Here is a wide view of the bullpen area, with Chloe O'Brian's workstation on the left, the second-floor catwalk at the far end, and the stairs leading to the catwalk and upstairs offices on the right.

CONFERENCE ROOM

CTU's main conference room is less private and secure than the Situation Room so it is used more for long-range planning, prep, and business sessions, while the Situation Room is used more for ultra-secret gatherings and breaking emergencies. Like the Situation Room, the conference room features a specially designed down-lighting fixture for illumination, and a 50-inch Panasonic Plasma screen on the wall, but it also has three, 20-inch Dell 2007WFP widescreen LCD monitors on the table. The room can seat up to 15 participants.

GROUND FLOOR

Interrogation Room

Conference Room

Corridor

Observation Room

Situation Room

INTERROGATION ROOM

The most controversial room at CTU is the interrogation room (pictured above, with CTU's polygraph system and truth drugs displayed). It is this room where suspects are secretly interrogated, sometimes in violation of the law in dire situations. The room has a one-way viewing window so officials can watch interrogations (as Jack Bauer is doing, below) whilst suspects are unaware.

MEDICAL CLINIC

Although CTU's medical staff routinely performs miracles, the clinic has also been the site of several tragedies, like Paul Raines' death and the murder of Tony Almeida. But perhaps none has been so senseless as the death of Erin Driscoll's daughter, Maya. A schizophrenic, Maya was brought to CTU's medical clinic to be monitored on Day 4 while her mother managed CTU's response to a major crisis. Confused, the frightened Maya slit her wrists and bled to death before the CTU medical staff discovered her.

SECOND FLOOR

Office

Directors Office

TONY ALMEIDA

Tony Almeida's life journey during his time at CTU traveled a zig-zag path of incredible highs and painful lows that finally culminated with his murder at the hands of Christopher Henderson. Almeida went from running CTU Los Angeles to being arrested for treason and needing a presidential pardon to get out of jail, and from seeing his career and marriage destroyed, to painstakingly rebuilding his life before having it snuffed out far too early. He grew up on the mean streets of South Chicago, earned multiple degrees in computer science, served in the Marine Corps, became an expert marksman and martial artist, and worked as a private industry computer analyst. Almeida was then recruited into CTU Los Angeles and rose through the ranks to become Deputy Director and then Special Agent in Charge, evolving into one of Jack Bauer's closest associates. During Day 4, with Bauer's urging, Almeida battled his way back from disgrace to play a central role in saving the lives of Bauer and Audrey Raines, helping Bauer stop Habib Marwan's terror plot, and along the way, reclaiming his marriage to Michelle Dessler.

TRUE LOVE

Tony Almeida and his wife, fellow CTU operative, Michelle Dessler, share a tender moment. A successful love affair is exceedingly rare in the world of espionage. They began working closely together at CTU during Day 2, married during the three years between Day 2 and Day 3, separated after Day 3 following Almeida's release from Federal prison, and then reconciled during Day 4 while working together once again at CTU.

FACT FILE

STATUS: Deceased

BIRTHPLACE: Chicago, Illinois

MARITAL STATUS: Was married to Michelle Dessler, but widowed at time of death

CHILDREN: None

EDUCATION:

- Master of Science, Computer Science—Stanford University
- Combined Bachelor of Engineering/Bachelor of Computer Science—San Diego State University

MILITARY:

- US Marine Corps—First Lieutenant
- Scout-Sniper School (3rd Marine Division)
- Surveillance & Target Acquision Platoon School (1st Marine Division)

EXPERIENCE:

- President of private security technology company
- Temporary assignment at CTU Los Angeles Domestic Unit, per order of Defense Secretary Heller
- Discharged from CTU for criminal act (later pardoned by President David Palmer)
- CTU (Los Angeles Domestic Unit)—Special Agent in Charge
- CTU (Los Angeles Domestic Unit)—Deputy Director
- Transmeta Corporation—Systems Validation Analyst

EXPERTISE: Certified Instructor, Krav Maga hand-to-hand combat defense system

INTERROGATION

During Day 4, Tony's skillful interrogation techniques played a crucial role in getting CTU solid leads on Habib Marwan's terror plans. He found Dina Araz's weakness—her desire to protect her son, Behrooz—and exploited it by using Behrooz's fate as a bargaining chip. Dina eventually gave in, and identified Marwan to CTU for the first time.

IN CHARGE

Tony Almeida's tactical skills, computer expertise, and experience allowed him to serve lengthy terms as a senior CTU official. He quickly rose to the rank of Deputy Director, and was eventually promoted to Special Agent in Charge, a post he held for several years, until his downfall during Day 3.

Mandy sent a photo of Tony to Michelle to prove she had captured him. Michelle followed protocol, notified her superiors, and initiated a rescue plan.

HOSTAGE

During Day 4, Tony is sent into the field in pursuit of a lead on Habib Marwan, and is taken hostage by the assassin Mandy (left). She attempts to use Tony as part of an elaborate ruse to make her escape, but Jack Bauer rescues him. Mandy, however, trades information on Marwan's location for a presidential pardon. Her current whereabouts are unclear.

BRUSH WITH DEATH

Almeida luckily survived being shot in the neck during Day 3. He was running CTU when a lead came up about the Cordilla Virus. CTU located a young man, Kyle Singer, who was unaware he might have been inadvertently transporting the virus. Almeida decided to bring Singer in personally, but one of Hector Salazar's men shot him and captured Kyle. Almeida was comatose for a few hours, but eventually resumed his post.

Tony Almeida lies seriously wounded after being shot in the neck by one of Salazar's thugs during Day 3 while attempting to track Kyle Singer.

Above, Tony Almeida rushes to Michelle Dessler's side seconds after her car exploded, only to find he is too late (below). Tony was seriously injured moments later when the car's fuel tank exploded.

CONSPIRACY VICTIMS

The pull of their former life was simply too strong for Tony and Michelle to escape. They were forced into Day 5's fatal conspiracy only because they helped Jack Bauer go into hiding 18 months earlier. All four people who helped Bauer—Almeida, Dessler, President David Palmer, and Chloe O'Brien—were targeted on Day 5. Palmer was assassinated, Dessler killed by a car bomb, and Almeida murdered at CTU by Christopher Henderson. Only O'Brien escaped, rescued by Bauer. The reason for their victimization was to prevent Palmer from exposing a plan to use acts of terror to trigger an American takeover of Asian oil interests, while misdirecting authorities.

TONY ALMEIDA

The irony of Tony Almeida's life is the fact that it ended violently shortly after he finally achieved true happiness living a quiet life with his wife, Michelle Dessler. They left CTU, started a private security firm, and were living in the suburbs when Day 5 began and they heard about David Palmer's assassination. Michelle made the fateful decision to go to CTU and assist with the investigation. But a car bomb killed her, and an ensuing explosion injured Tony, sending him to CTU for medical attention and protection. He subsequently learned of the scheme to wipe out everyone connected to Jack Bauer's disappearance, and Christopher Henderson's role in those events. Lacking the cold nerve of a killer, his half-hearted attempt to murder Henderson at CTU's medical clinic led to his demise when he dropped his guard and was taken by surprise.

Almeida learns from Stephen Saunders that he is holding Michelle hostage.

Almeida makes his move, forcing a guard to help him free Saunders' daughter from custody.

DOWNFALL

During Day 3, Tony faced the ultimate dilemma: duty or family? When Stephen Saunders kidnapped Michelle and used her as leverage to manipulate Almeida into helping him slip CTU's net and return his daughter to him, Almeida chose to put his wife's safety ahead of his country's. Dessler was eventually rescued, and Saunders captured, but Tony's actions got him fired from CTU, arrested, and charged with treason.

Tony Almeida is apprehended and prevented from completing his plan to free Michelle.

Almeida leaves CTU in Federal custody, accused of treason and facing life in prison, or even execution.

Tony hesitates (top), uncertain if he can murder Henderson in cold blood, while Henderson has no such qualms.

TONY'S DEATH

Tony Almeida never shared Jack Bauer's cold, dispassionate ability to kill under particular circumstances, and for this he paid the ultimate price. Trapped in CTU's medical clinic on Day 5 with the man who killed his wife, during the Sentox nerve gas attack on CTU, Almeida eventually decided to exact revenge on Christopher Henderson by injecting him with an overdose of hyoscine-pentothal, the drug used by CTU interrogators to make Henderson talk. Almeida hesitated, however, and Henderson jammed the needle into Tony's chest. Almeida died moments later in Jack Bauer's arms, as Henderson escaped.

Tony lies dying as the deadly dose of hyoscine-pentothal circulates through his system.

Once again, Jack Bauer is forced to watch a friend die in his arms—this time, Tony Almeida. Bauer arrived too late to prevent Henderson's murderous escape, and can only comfort his friend and ally in his final moments.

MICHELLE DESSLER

Even during the most difficult moments navigating between her complicated relationship with Tony Almeida and her CTU duties, Michelle Dessler routinely displayed matchless courage, loyalty, leadership, and clarity of thought. These traits were best illustrated during Day 3 when Michelle knowingly and without hesitation entered the quarantined Chandler Plaza Hotel without a biohazard suit—risking likely exposure to a deadly virus—in order to obtain crucial evidence. Yet, twice she sacrificed her career growth to be with Tony—the first time when he was imprisoned in Washington State, she had herself transferred to be near him; and the second time, after Day 4, when she left CTU to rebuild their marriage. After graduating with a Computer Science degree from the University of California, Davis, and working in the computer industry, she was recruited to CTU due to her proficiency in computer systems security, and quickly rose from a low-level job as an Internet Protocol Manager to Special Agent in Charge. But, by that point, her relationship with Tony had become the priority in her life, and things were falling nicely into place for the couple when she was murdered in a car-bomb explosion early on Day 5.

REUNITED

Michelle visits Tony in the hospital on Day 3, shortly after Tony emerged from a coma after being shot. It was a rare moment of release for Michelle, who had to wait out Almeida's surgery while remaining at her post at CTU. With Tony incapacitated, Michelle had to assume his command.

FACT FILE

STATUS: Deceased

BIRTHPLACE: Classified

MARITAL STATUS: Re-married to Tony Almeida (at time of death)

CHILDREN: None

RELATIVES: Danny Dessler (brother)

EXPERIENCE:
- Associate Special Agent in Charge, CTU Division
- Intelligence Agent, CTU Los Angeles, Domestic Unit
- Internet Protocol Manager, CTU Los Angeles, Domestic Unit
- DARPA—High Confidence Systems Working Group
- National Institute of Standards & Technology, Computer Security Division

EDUCATION:
Bachelor of Science, Computer Science—University of California, Davis

COMPUTER EXPERTISE:
- Built IPSec architecture
- Attacks scripts
- Computer vulnerabilities
- Intrusion detection
- Penetration testing operational security
- Viruses

A grim Michelle Dessler takes charge to make sure no one enters or leaves the Chandler Plaza Hotel to avoid spread of the deadly virus.

HORROR UNLEASHED

On Day 3, guests at the Chandler Plaza Hotel were exposed to the Cordilla Virus as part of Stephen Saunders' terror plot. Michelle was tasked with heading up the field team at the scene, but she entered the building without a biohazard suit. She failed to stop exposure, and then grappled with the horrific task of informing hotel guests of their impending fate, preventing them from fleeing, and supplying those who wanted them with suicide capsules. Miraculously, Michelle was among the small number of people who survived, due to natural immunity to the virus.

Michelle interrogates Marcus Alvers, and tries to force him to tell her where he has distributed the virus.

Michelle attempts to calm and control hotel guests as the horrible truth about the spread of the virus is revealed.

HUSBAND AND WIFE

For all its tragedy, Day 4 also had a positive impact on Michelle's life. That was the day Tony returned to CTU following his painful fall from grace, only to find Michelle running things. Initially suspicious of Tony given his recent behavior, she kept her distance. But eventually she began working closely with him once again and her trust in him was gradually restored, so that by Day 5, they had reunited.

Michelle Dessler and Tony Almeida pictured here in the last moments of their lives together as Day 5 dawns. Moments later, she was dead, Almeida was badly injured, and their love story was over.

LIFE THREATENING

Live video footage streamed directly to Tony shows Michelle being threatened with death by Stephen Saunders after her abduction during Day 3. The tactic, designed to force Almeida's cooperation, worked perfectly. Ignoring Dessler's pleas, Almeida agreed to help get Saunders' daughter released from CTU custody in exchange for sparing Dessler's life.

NINA MYERS

For several years, Nina Myers appeared to be Jack Bauer's closest ally at CTU, and for a brief time, she was also his lover. After Day 1, that history lay in ruins, nothing more than an elaborate lie constructed by a ruthless double-agent—Nina Myers. She not only betrayed Bauer, she also killed his wife, and in the long run, paved the way for her own death at Bauer's hand during Day 3, some four and a half years later. Prior to Day 1, she was officially listed as highly educated, from the Boston area, with a background of working in private industry and government before coming to CTU to serve as Assistant Special Agent in Charge under Christopher Henderson. After Henderson left CTU, she became Bauer's Chief of Staff and worked closely with him for about seven years as a mole inside CTU. However, after Day 1, CTU officially classified Myers' record, leaving it unclear how much of her resumé prior to CTU is accurate. All that is known for certain is that she worked for an unnamed criminal organization based in Germany, used the alias of Yelena, was fluent in several languages, and was a deadly killer.

ULTIMATE BETRAYAL

Her cover blown, Nina Myers gags a terrified Teri Bauer near the end of Day 1 in a CTU Tech Room as she plots her escape. Teri accidentally overheard Nina speaking to her handler, and for that, she was murdered in cold blood. Soon after, Myers attempted to shoot her way out of CTU, but was captured by Jack Bauer and arrested before he learned about the murder.

AGENDA

On Day 1, Nina Myers aided the Drazen family. She did so not out of loyalty to the Drazens or concern for their grudge against Jack Bauer, but simply because her mysterious German employers loaned her to the Drazens. It's clear Myers spied on CTU for many years, on several different cases, and that the Drazens were merely her latest job. Since she served widely divergent causes, its doubtful Myers had a political agenda. More likely, she lived her double life purely for financial gain.

IN CUSTODY

Jack Bauer recaptures Nina Myers after forcing her to lead him to her contact with the Second Wave terrorist organization during Day 2. Bauer discovered Myers had sold CTU schematics to the terror group, and had her released from prison to help him foil the organization's nuclear bomb plot. She led Bauer to her contact and tried to escape, but Bauer stopped her.

Nina Myers and Jack Bauer face off once again in Mexico on Day 3, after Myers captures Bauer, unsure of his true agenda.

UNDERCOVER

Myers resurfaces on Day 3 in Mexico, attempting to act as a broker to purchase the Cordilla Virus from Michael Amador. There, she finds herself competing with Jack Bauer, ostensibly representing the Salazar brothers. This time, Bauer is the one who is deep undercover, representing himself as having abandoned CTU. He eventually recaptures Myers, and brings her back to CTU, where they eventually have their final encounter.

As part of her cruel game, Nina Myers attempts to kiss Jack Bauer, hoping to somehow discern his true intentions.

THE MURDER OF JACK BAUER

Nina Myers holds Jack Bauer prisoner during Day 2, planning to execute him momentarily. She is waiting to hear back on her demand from President David Palmer for a pardon in advance for the act she is about to commit. The delay in Palmer's response, however, saved Bauer's life as he moved into a position where a CTU sniper could take Myers down while she hesitated.

SELF-DEFENSE?

Nina Myers' ending came on Day 3 when Jack Bauer cornered her in the same Tech Room where she killed Teri Bauer. Bauer testified that the wounded Myers reached for her gun, so he shot her dead. The security camera view was obscured, and only Bauer knows for sure what transpired.

CHLOE O'BRIAN

Since transferring to CTU's Los Angeles Domestic Unit from the Washington/Baltimore Domestic Unit some time prior to Day 3, senior analyst Chloe O'Brian has proven to be a uniquely gifted data analyst and programmer, a key player in CTU's efforts to thwart terror plots, and a loyal supporter of Jack Bauer. Indeed, O'Brian's intense loyalty to Bauer, other colleagues, and the greater mission, rather than official CTU protocols, has periodically jeopardized her career. During Day 3, she cared for Chase Edmunds' baby, and covered for him even though her job was threatened. At the end of Day 4, she was one of the few people to be entrusted with knowledge that Jack Bauer was alive—information that almost got her killed on Day 5. That same day, despite official disapproval, she illicitly helped Bauer investigate David Palmer's assassination, and assisted the effort to bring President Logan to justice. Late in Day 6, she revealed she was pregnant.

PERSONAL RELATIONSHIP

Chloe O'Brian's ex-husband, Morris O'Brian— a brilliant engineer and recovering alcoholic— rejoined her late in Day 5 when she brought him to CTU as a freelance analyst. Late on Day 5, he comforted Chloe as she processed the shock of Edgar Stiles' death. By Day 6, Morris was working as a CTU analyst, battling with Chloe right up until he learned she was carrying his child.

DISMISSED

O'Brian is arrested on Day 4 on orders from CTU Director Erin Driscoll after she is caught helping Jack Bauer without authorization. Driscoll later offered O'Brian a chance to resign as an alternative to prosecution, and O'Brian took the offer and left CTU. A few hours later, however, Michelle Dessler replaced Driscoll, and summoned O'Brian back to CTU. Chloe complied despite reservations, after Dessler made it clear that the success of Jack Bauer's mission required her help.

DESPERATE SITUATION

Jack Bauer calms a terrified Chloe O'Brian moments after they are reunited at an abandoned oil refinery early on Day 5. O'Brian realized that she, like everyone who knew Jack Bauer was alive, was being targeted for death. So she contacted Bauer, bringing an end to the fiction concocted almost 20 months earlier at the end of Day 4 that he was dead, and brought him out of hiding. As the Day 5 crisis unfolded, Bauer found O'Brian, saved her from thugs working for the conspiracy that murdered President David Palmer, and killed the assassin who shot Palmer.

UNAUTHORIZED

Chloe O'Brian works with Bill Buchanan from Buchanan's home after they left CTU following the agency's takeover by the Department of Homeland Security on Day 5. Buchanan was unjustly blamed for a breach of security at CTU, and O'Brian was relieved of duty and detained. Buchanan then went home, and O'Brian escaped custody to help him track Christopher Henderson and crucial evidence implicating President Charles Logan. Before being apprehended, she managed to access CTU satellite data, find the evidence's location, and pass crucial information about the courier carrying it to Jack Bauer.

TRAGIC LOSS

Despite their mutual social awkwardness and periodic confrontations, Chloe O'Brian and Edgar Stiles developed a close bond during their time working together at CTU in the period beginning shortly before Day 4 and climaxing, sadly, with Edgar's death in the Sentox nerve gas attack on CTU during Day 5. O'Brian was profoundly impacted by his untimely death.

EDGAR STILES & THE CTU ANALYSTS

On the surface, Edgar Stiles was overweight, shy, and lacking in social skills. But his photographic memory and superior computer data retrieval skills made him a priceless asset to the CTU team. In particular, during Day 4, Stiles stepped to the forefront as the unlikely hero of the nuclear power plant meltdown crisis initiated by Habib Marwan. He was the one analyst at CTU who figured out a programming methodology for commanding 98 nuclear power plants around the country to shut down before they could reach critical mass and melt down. He stopped all but one meltdown—at St. Gabriel Island. However, that tragedy resulted in the death of Edgar's mother, and left him alone in the world. He continued at CTU, and eventually developed an awkward friendship with his colleague and supervisor, Chloe O'Brian. Stiles' life sadly came to an end during the Day 5 Sentox nerve gas attack on CTU.

FACT FILE

STATUS: Deceased

BIRTHPLACE: Classified

MARITAL STATUS: Single at time of death

CHILDREN: None

RELATIVES: Lucy Stiles (mother, deceased)

EXPERIENCE:
- CTU Intelligence Analyst, Los Angeles Domestic Unit
- CTU Internet Protocol Manager, Los Angeles Domestic Unit

EDUCATION:
Bachelor of Science, Computer Applications (with honors)—New York University

COMPUTER EXPERTISE:
Operating systems, distributed systems, informational retrieval and wireless networks.

CLUED UP

During Day 4, Edgar Stiles worked closely with CTU analyst Sarah Gavin (pictured left), and even while struggling to prevent meltdowns at multiple nuclear power plants (seen on his monitor, above), he saved Gavin from an espionage charge. The real mole, Marianne Taylor, attempted to frame Gavin, but Stiles discovered the truth and exposed Taylor as the true threat.

LOCKED OUT

Edgar Stiles' kindness and concern for others ironically led to his death during the Sentox nerve gas attack on CTU during Day 5. As the attack began, Stiles left his station to go searching for a missing colleague, Carrie Bendis. By the time he returned, the CTU Situation Room had been locked down. Stiles collapsed and died to the horror of his colleagues watching from the other side of the sealed glass partition.

MILO PRESSMAN

Pressman was a computer language expert with particular proficiency in decoding encrypted data. He played crucial roles aiding Jack Bauer on Day 1 and Day 6, and acquitted himself well in the field on Day 6, saving Marilyn Bauer's life. On Day 1, as a consultant for CTU, he decoded data on Richard Walsh's key card and helped Bauer identify Alexis Drazen's involvement in the plot. Later, Pressman joined CTU as a Senior Analyst, and transferred for a time to CTU's Denver Domestic Unit. He returned to Los Angeles prior to Day 6, and became romantically interested in Nadia Yassir that day. Near the end of Day 6, he saved her life at the cost of his own—he told the Chinese commandos who invaded CTU that he was in charge, and they promptly shot him dead.

JAMEY FARRELL

Prior to Day 1, Farrell was one of CTU's key data programmers. On Day 1, however, she was exposed as a mole operating under Ira Gaines' control, committing the crime out of financial need. After her exposure, she became distraught and apparently committed suicide. However, it was later revealed that Farrell was actually murdered by Nina Myers to prevent her from exposing Gaines' link to the Drazens.

SCOTT BAYLOR

Baylor was the CTU data analyst who discovered Richard Walsh's keycard was secretly encoded with data connected to the threat against David Palmer—which proved that CTU had a mole in its midst in Day 1. Rightly assuming that his life was in danger, Baylor handed the keycard to Walsh, and made plans to disappear. But he was betrayed by CTU mole, Jamey Farrell, and shot dead before he could escape.

CARRIE TURNER

Michelle Dessler had bad blood with CTU analyst Turner when she arrived at CTU during Day 2, because Turner had previously broken up the marriage of Michelle's brother. Turner began reporting to Ryan Chappelle on Dessler's apparent attempts to aid Jack Bauer outside official channels, and at one point even tried to blackmail Tony Almeida into promoting her over Dessler. She left CTU at the end of Day 2.

PAULA SCHAEFFER

Schaeffer joined CTU on Day 2, and immediately proved her worth, despite battling fears about the nuclear threat in LA. When CTU was bombed, she was gravely injured and CTU's encrypted data on the nuclear threat was in danger of being lost. Against doctors' advice George Mason ordered that Schaeffer be revived to decrypt the remaining information. She did this heroically before succumbing to her injuries.

ADAM KAUFMAN

Kaufman joined CTU between Day 2 and Day 3, but repeatedly clashed with Chloe O'Brian and Kim Bauer. On Day 3, he found Kim after she had been tied up by Gael Ortega, which led to CTU's discovery that Ortega was operating undercover at CTU on a secret mission for Jack Bauer. Kaufman later learned that his sister had been infected with the Cordilla Virus. He eventually left CTU.

SARAH GAVIN

During Day 4, Gavin was set up by Marianne Taylor, who was working as a mole at CTU. Taylor manufactured evidence, implicating Gavin as the spy. Gavin was arrested and, on orders from Erin Driscoll, briefly tortured. Edgar Stiles proved Gavin's innocence, but then she demanded a promotion as payment for her suffering. Michelle Dessler refused her demand, dismissed her, and reinstated the suspended Chloe O'Brian instead.

MARIANNE TAYLOR

Taylor was a consultant with a past relationship with Curtis Manning when she came to CTU on Day 4. Henry Powell hired her to infiltrate CTU to aid him as he helped Habib Marwan use the Dobson Override Device. She was eventually exposed and captured by Manning. Taylor then agreed to help Manning locate files at Powell's office. There, however, she was killed by one of Marwan's henchmen.

SPENSER WOLFF

Wolff was a CTU analyst used as a pawn on Day 5 by Walt Cummings, President Logan's Chief of Staff. He was manipulated into accessing secure data and unwittingly allowing an assassin into CTU before being discovered by Chloe O'Brian. Wolff later attempted to redeem himself by helping CTU override a security system at an important location. Despite that assistance, he was fired for his duplicity.

CARRIE BENDIS

On Day 5, Bendis contributed to the removal of Lynn McGill as head of CTU, but later lost her life. After arguing with Bendis, McGill's downward spiral due to the pressure of the day began, leading to his eventual removal. Later, Bendis investigated a problem with the CTU ventilation system, and was murdered there by the terrorist Ostroff, who planted Sentox nerve gas in the facility.

SHARI ROTHENBERG

A low-level analyst with a history of filing sexual harassment claims, Rothenberg joined CTU Los Angeles during Day 5. Her scientific knowledge allowed CTU to stop Vladimir Bierko from releasing Sentox nerve gas at the Wilshire Gas Company, and she discovered that Chloe O'Brian was improperly working to help Jack Bauer. Chloe later blackmailed Rothenberg into helping her escape which later led to Rothenberg's arrest.

VALERIE HARRIS

When Homeland Security briefly absorbed CTU late in Day 5, Valerie Harris was appointed to step into Chloe O'Brian's shoes as a senior analyst. She was assigned to track Audrey Raines, and helped discover Raines and Jack Bauer were working outside channels to find evidence against President Logan. She also discovered that Shari Rothenberg helped Chloe escape custody during this period, and had Rothenberg arrested.

MORRIS O'BRIAN

O'Brian is Chloe O'Brian's ex-husband, an analytical genius, and recovering alcoholic. His career has ranged from senior data analyst to shoe salesman. He first came to CTU as a consultant on Day 5, and helped Chloe cover for Jack Bauer's unorthodox actions. On Day 6, he was abducted and tortured by Abu Fayed into building a nuclear bomb trigger, but later played a central role in helping CTU handle the threat.

BILL BUCHANAN

Bill Buchanan is a veteran CTU official who, until recently, served as Special Agent in Charge of the Los Angeles Domestic Unit. Buchanan started with CTU as a field agent in New York, and later served as an intelligence analyst and senior agent in CTU's Seattle Division Office, and as Associate Agent in charge of CTU's Los Angeles Division office. He took over as head of the Los Angeles Domestic Unit prior to Day 4, when CTU's command team was reorganized, and served as Special Agent in Charge for a lengthy period, although he was forced to yield to Lynn McGill's command during Day 5, and was even detained by McGill at one point. Later, after he reassumed command and CTU was hit by a deadly terrorist attack, the agency was taken over by the Department of Homeland Security (DHS), and Buchanan was ousted in favor of a DHS official named Karen Hayes, who eventually became a supporter of Buchanan, and later, his wife. After Day 5, Buchanan was reinstated as CTU chief, but on Day 6, he was fired in a political power play. He later risked his life to help Jack Bauer save his nephew, Josh, and was then expected to retire.

PERSONNEL DEPARTMENT

Part of Bill Buchanan's job involves managing the strong personalities and conflicts that permeate his CTU staff. Buchanan has had his own relationships to navigate, and knows better than anyone that CTU is made up of flawed human beings engaged in complex relationships while under great stress. Sometimes, that means showing a soft side, as pictured here, when he gave Chloe O'Brian a picture of herself with Edgar Stiles. Other times, it can mean making cold, difficult decisions, such as ordering Nadia Yassir to be interrogated during Day 6.

SECTION 112

On Day 5, a series of questionable command decisions and paranoid behavior by Lynn McGill, including a directive to arrest Bill Buchanan, led CTU staff to question McGill's fitness for command. Eventually, agent Curtis Manning made the extremely rare decision to invoke the Section 112 clause of the CTU charter. The clause permits the second-ranking agent in a CTU office to remove the ranking agent from command if he believes that individual to be mentally unfit. Manning invoked the clause, had McGill detained, informed Division Command of his actions, and Buchanan was soon reinstated.

PARTNERS

Bill Buchanan confronts Karen Hayes on Day 5, shortly after Hayes moved to absorb CTU into the Department of Homeland Security, which lead to Buchanan's temporary dismissal. Hayes and Buchanan got off to a rocky start, but she eventually began cooperating with him to secure proof of President Charles Logan's duplicitous manipulations of the day's events. Some time between Day 5 and Day 6, she and Buchanan began a romantic relationship and got married.

FACT FILE

AGE: 51

MARITAL STATUS:
Married to Karen Hayes

CHILDREN: None

GOVERNMENT EXPERIENCE:
- CTU—Special Agent in Charge, Los Angeles Domestic Unit
- CTU Los Angeles Division Office—Associate Special Agent in Charge
- CTU Seattle Division Office—Senior Agent
- CTU Seattle Division Office—Intelligence Analyst
- CTU—Field Agent, New York Domestic Unit

EDUCATION:
Bachelor of Arts, English Literature— Brown University

THE RETURN

Bill Buchanan led a CTU team to a bittersweet reunion with Jack Bauer at Ellis Airfield on Day 6, after Chinese authorities released Bauer. Buchanan immediately had the unfortunate duty of informing Bauer that his new-found freedom would be short-lived—Bauer was released as part of a deal brokered by President Wayne Palmer to turn him over to terrorist Abu Fayed in return for valuable intelligence.

CONFRONTATION

Buchanan immediately butted heads with CTU Division executive Lynn McGill on Day 5, when McGill came to supervise CTU. Throughout the day, McGill made a series of poor decisions and questioned the loyalty of senior-level staff members, including Buchanan. He unjustly had Buchanan relieved of duty and detained (below), impeding the investigation into the Sentox nerve gas plot—a plot that would ironically strike the heart of CTU, and end McGill's life a short time later.

BACK IN ACTION

Shortly after being fired from his position as Special Agent in Charge at CTU on Day 6, Bill Buchanan is called upon to help Jack Bauer save his nephew, Josh. Pulling a gun on the pilot, Bauer commandeers the CTU helicopter that was meant to take him and Buchanan back to CTU. Jack is extremely grateful when Buchanan offers to fly the chopper to save the innocent boy.

CTU: COMMAND AND CONTROL

CTU SENIOR OFFICIALS

Given the dangerous, stressful, and often political nature of counter-terrorism work, it's not surprising that numerous senior officials have held the job of commanding CTU over the years. Changes usually occur when officials are killed or injured, fired or arrested for misconduct, step down for personal reasons, or are usurped for political reasons. Generally, the Chief of Staff takes over if there is a change, either temporarily or permanently, but District or Division executives can assume direct control themselves. On some occasions, officials from other agencies have also taken the reigns, such as Defense Secretary James Heller on Day 4 and Homeland Security official Karen Hayes on Day 5.

George Mason

George Mason's story is a tragic one—he rose to a high-ranking position within CTU, was linked to corruption by Jack Bauer on Day 1, and then heroically sacrificed his life to save others on Day 2. Mason was CTU's Los Angeles District Director on Day 1when he butted heads with Bauer before helping him stop the hit on David Palmer. But Day 2 was the end of the road for Mason. As Special Agent in Charge, he was leading CTU's investigation of the nuclear terror threat when he was exposed to a fatal dose of Plutonium. He quit, but still tried to help CTU find the terrorists' nuclear device. He ended up doing more than help—saving hundreds of thousands of lives by completing a suicide mission instead of Jack.

An already-dying George Mason takes over for Jack Bauer on a one-way mission to crash a nuclear warhead into the desert on Day 2.

RICHARD WALSH

Walsh was CTU's Administrative Director heading into Day 1, and was one of Jack Bauer's earliest mentors in the agency. On Day 1, convinced there was a mole operating inside CTU, he procured information on who that might be in the form of an encrypted CTU keycard. When he was ambushed, he called Bauer to help, and forfeited his own life to help Bauer get the data back to CTU.

JACK BAUER

Bauer was Special Agent in Charge at CTU Los Angeles heading into Day 1, replaced for a time, then reinstated, but then placed under George Mason's authority through Day 2. He temporarily resumed the lead role late in Day 3, but left CTU before Day 4 to join the Defense Department. Since then, Bauer has collaborated with CTU on a provisional basis, but not in a senior management role.

ALBERTA GREEN

After Jack Bauer went rogue on Day 1, Alberta Green, a CTU Division Director, took over CTU Los Angeles. Determined to locate Bauer, she clashed with Tony Almeida and Nina Myers, convinced they were helping him. She interrogated Bauer when he resurfaced, but Senator David Palmer demanded Bauer's reinstatement. Ryan Chappelle complied, but brought in George Mason to supervise, Green transferred out.

TONY ALMEIDA

Almeida, previously CTU's Deputy Director, took over as Special Agent in Charge on Day 2, after George Mason's death. He was running CTU on Day 3 when he was wounded. He was later arrested and fired following his attempt to save Michelle Dessler's life. He returned to run CTU temporarily after Erin Driscoll resigned on Day 4, then quit for good. He was murdered by Christopher Henderson on Day 5.

RYAN CHAPPELLE

CTU's Regional Division Director Chappelle was a bureaucrat who oversaw the agency on authority from District Command on Days 1, 2, and 3. His obsession with protocol was a hindrance, particularly on Day 2. On Day 3, he helped track Stephen Saunders, who then threatened to murder thousands of people unless Chappelle was executed. President David Palmer reluctantly ordered Jack Bauer to carry out the deed.

BRAD HAMMOND

Hammond, a Division Supervisor, investigated irregularities at CTU on Days 2 and 3. On Day 2, he tried shutting CTU down after it was bombed, and also investigated Ryan Chappelle's disappearance. On Day 3, Hammond interrogated Tony Almeida after he appeared to help Stephen Saunders, but released him to run tactical operations during the Cordilla Virus threat. Later he had Almeida arrested for treason.

ERIN DRISCOLL

Driscoll was a CTU Division official who took over as Special Agent in Charge prior to Day 4. She had a no-nonsense approach, even firing Jack Bauer early in her tenure. She managed the agency through the first half of the Day 4 crisis, but became distracted when her daughter, a schizophrenic, was brought to the CTU medical clinic. When her daughter committed suicide, Driscoll left CTU.

LYNN MCGILL

Divisional executive Lynn McGill came to CTU Los Angeles on Day 5 to supervise the nerve gas investigation. He proved inexperienced, compromised security, exhibited signs of paranoia, and even had Bill Buchanan detained at one point. McGill was eventually relieved of duty, but redeemed himself following the nerve gas attack on the facility by heroically venting CTU of the deadly gas, at the cost of his own life.

KAREN HAYES

Hayes, a former FBI agent and Division Director for the Department of Homeland Security (DHS), was given the task of supervising the absorption of CTU by DHS on Day 5. After initially butting heads, she worked with her future husband, Bill Buchanan, to investigate President Charles Logan. By Day 6, she was a senior advisor to President Wayne Palmer, but by the end of the day, events forced her into retirement.

NADIA YASSIR

Yassir came to CTU Los Angeles after Day 5, and quickly rose to the position of Bill Buchanan's Chief of Staff. After he was fired late on Day 6, she was promoted to Special Agent in Charge. She took control of CTU's attempt to recover the FB sub-circuit board to avoid a confrontation with the Russians, and also helped Jack Bauer end the bloody takeover of CTU by Chinese commandos.

MICHELLE DESSLER

Dessler was a computer security expert who rose to serve as Chief of Staff before twice taking over the top position at CTU Los Angeles—first as Associate Special Agent in Charge, and later, Acting Special Agent in Charge, both times replacing the man she loved, Tony Almeida. On Day 3, she replaced Almeida after he was shot, serving under Ryan Chappelle's authority, and later yielding the position back to Almeida. On Day 4, after Erin Driscoll stepped down, Almeida took charge until a new director could arrive from Division. That Director was Dessler—his former wife. Reporting to Bill Buchanan, she helped manage CTU through Day 4, and was one of the people who helped Jack Bauer disappear. She then left CTU to rebuild her life with Almeida, but was murdered on Day 5.

BILL BUCHANAN

Buchanan was one of the longest serving Directors in CTU history. He took over first as Regional Director on Day 4, and later became Special Agent in Charge following Michelle Dessler, and served in that job most of the time after Day 4 through Day 6. On Day 5, Lynn McGill unjustly fired him. He was reinstated, but later that day, and again on Day 6, Buchanan fell victim to political scapegoating. On Day 5, he was dismissed to pin blame for the security breach that led to the nerve gas attack on CTU, but later got his job back. On Day 6, his wife, Karen Hayes, was forced to fire Buchanan to limit political fallout related to the release years earlier of terrorist Abu Fayed. Later that day, Vice President Noah Daniels forced both Buchanan and Hayes to quietly retire.

CTU: COMMAND AND CONTROL

CTU DIRECTOR OF FIELD OPERATIONS

The job of Director of Field Operations (DFO) is a high-ranking position at CTU. The DFO is the agency's top field commander, with tactical control over both TAC units and general deployments of agents in combat, and usually the first person into the line of fire. The DFO's command in the field is subject only to the authority of CTU's Special Agent in Charge or Chief of Staff, and even then, when under attack, he has the right to make whatever tactical decisions he thinks best. Those holding the position are highly likely to be military or SWAT veterans with several years of field experience, martial arts, and firearms expertise.

DFOs

Christopher Henderson was CTU's DFO prior to Day 1, and later recruited Jack Bauer. Bauer served as DFO a few times through Day 3, before being fired by Erin Driscoll. She named Ronnie Lobell DFO, and he held the position until being killed early on Day 4. He was replaced by Curtis Manning, who was DFO until Day 6 when, tragically, he was killed in a confrontation with Bauer. Mike Doyle then took over, but was injured in a bomb blast late in the day.

MIKE DOYLE

After Curtis Manning's death, Mike Doyle took over as DFO on Day 6. He led the assault on the Russian Consulate, and then alternately worked with Jack Bauer and chased him down when Bauer went rogue. He later ran the operation to turn Josh Bauer over to Phillip Bauer in return for recovering the FB sub-circuit board, but the device was rigged. It blew up in Doyle's hands, damaging his eyesight—the extent was not immediately clear.

CURTIS MANNING

Manning's life ended on Day 6 when terrorist Hamri Al-Assad came between him and his friend, Jack Bauer. Manning had a grudge against Al-Assad dating back to Operation Desert Storm. On Day 6, Al-Assad was offered a pardon in return for helping CTU's investigation. When Manning learned of the offer, he attempted to kill Al-Assad. Bauer ordered him to stand down, and when Manning refused, Bauer reluctantly shot him to death.

CTU CHIEFS OF STAFF

At all CTU Domestic Units, the Chief of Staff serves as second-in-command, serving under the Special Agent in Charge. The Chief of Staff frequently runs CTU when the Special Agent is in the field or otherwise unavailable, and often takes over the top job if the Special Agent is removed or killed. Over the years, Nina Myers, Tony Almeida, Michelle Dessler, and Nadia Yassir have held the job through major crisis periods, and at different times, all but Myers were elevated to the job of Special Agent in Charge. The person holding the position has a high security clearance, which is what made Nina Myers particularly dangerous as a mole operating inside CTU through Day 1. Yassir, conversely, was a loyal agent, but had her clearance temporarily and unfairly downgraded on Day 6 due to her Muslim background, making it nearly impossible to do her job.

DEADLY BUSINESS

In the years between Day 1 and Day 6, only five people have officially filled the position of Chief of Staff at CTU Los Angeles, although sometimes, the position has been vacant, and at other times, others have handled the duties, such as Day 4, when Curtis Manning filled in, while maintaining the title of Assistant Director of Field Operations. Sadly, Manning and all the others who held the job since Day 1 are now deceased, with the exception of Nadia Yassir. Of the others: Nina Myers was exposed as a traitor and killed by Jack Bauer on Day 3; Tony Almeida left CTU, but was murdered by Christopher Henderson on Day 5; and his wife, Michelle Dessler, was killed in a car bomb at Henderson's behest at the beginning of Day 5.

TRAGIC NEWS

At 11:05 p.m. on Day 2, in front of an image of a mushroom cloud bursting over the Mojave Desert, Tony Almeida has the difficult task of informing CTU staff that George Mason has died, and urges them to carry on through the crisis. As Chief of Staff, Almeida immediately assumed all of Mason's duties.

NADIA YASSIR

As Chief of Staff on Day 6, Nadia Yassir was brutally tested under fire. She was falsely accused of collaborating with terrorists, roughly interrogated by Mike Doyle (left, top), and when cleared of any wrongdoing she was suddenly reinstated to active duty. Next, despite her own doubts, she was elevated to Acting Special Agent in Charge when Bill Buchanan was dismissed, and after forming a personal relationship with Milo Pressman (left, bottom), she watched helplessly as Pressman took a bullet meant for her. By the end of Day 6, Yassir realized the need to pay less attention to protocol, and more attention to her gut instincts.

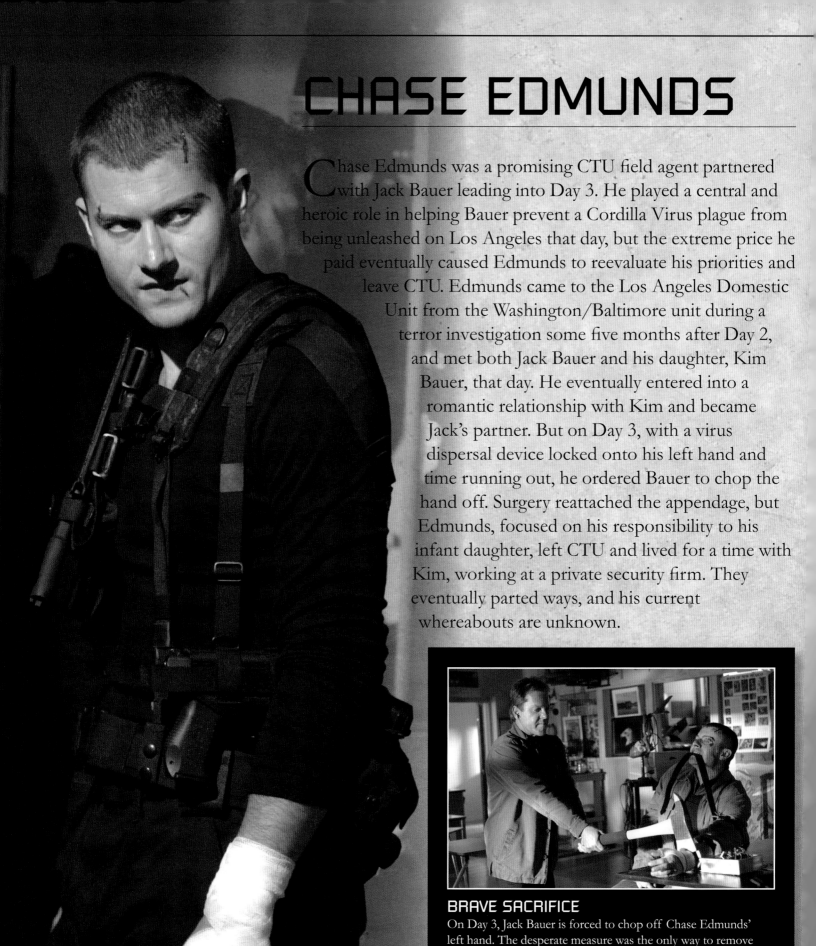

CHASE EDMUNDS

Chase Edmunds was a promising CTU field agent partnered with Jack Bauer leading into Day 3. He played a central and heroic role in helping Bauer prevent a Cordilla Virus plague from being unleashed on Los Angeles that day, but the extreme price he paid eventually caused Edmunds to reevaluate his priorities and leave CTU. Edmunds came to the Los Angeles Domestic Unit from the Washington/Baltimore unit during a terror investigation some five months after Day 2, and met both Jack Bauer and his daughter, Kim Bauer, that day. He eventually entered into a romantic relationship with Kim and became Jack's partner. But on Day 3, with a virus dispersal device locked onto his left hand and time running out, he ordered Bauer to chop the hand off. Surgery reattached the appendage, but Edmunds, focused on his responsibility to his infant daughter, left CTU and lived for a time with Kim, working at a private security firm. They eventually parted ways, and his current whereabouts are unknown.

BRAVE SACRIFICE

On Day 3, Jack Bauer is forced to chop off Chase Edmunds' left hand. The desperate measure was the only way to remove the locked device containing the Cordilla Virus from Edmunds' body before it could release the deadly strain after courier Arthur Rabens locked the device to his arm. When efforts to remove it proved futile, Edmunds demanded Bauer cut off the hand, and he did so—rushing the device into a sealed refrigerator, saving thousands of lives.

FACT FILE

AGE: Classified

BIRTHPLACE: Classified

MARITAL STATUS: Single

CHILDREN: One daughter, Angela

EDUCATION:
- Washington D.C. MPD—ERT basic training
- Washington D.C. MPD—Police Academy Special Forces Operations Training Course

GOVERNMENT EXPERIENCE:
- Field Operations Agent, CTU Los Angeles Domestic Unit
- Field Operations Agent, CTU Washington/Baltimore Domestic Unit
- Emergency Response Team, Washington D.C. MPD

AWARDS:
- Honors in Tactical Shooting, MPDC SWAT competition
- Commendations in Weapons and Field Reconnaissance

CURRENT WHEREABOUTS:
Unknown

GOING DARK

Chase Edmunds gets the drop on Mexican agent Rafael Gutierrez after sneaking into Mexico in pursuit of Jack Bauer. Edmunds had gone dark, out of communication with CTU, and was therefore unaware of Bauer's undercover mission in Mexico and the real reasons behind Bauer's prison breakout of Ramon Salazar. He cautiously approached Gutierrez, and quickly confirmed he was an ally, but before Gutierrez could put him in touch with CTU to fill him in on Bauer's mission, Gutierrez was shot dead by snipers working for the Salazars. Edmunds was captured moments later following a brief chase.

COMPLICATED AFFAIR

His relationship with Kim Bauer complicated Chase Edmunds' professional and personal lives greatly on Day 3. Because he was Jack Bauer's partner, Kim Bauer insisted Edmunds keep their relationship secret. Edmunds also kept important information from Kim—the fact that he had an infant daughter. When the truth came out on all sides during Day 3, it strained relations among the trio. By the end of the day, however, having witnessed Edmunds' bravery and dedication under fire, Bauer came to respect his daughter's decision, and Kim forgave Edmunds. The couple tried to make a go of it together after Day 3, but eventually went their separate ways.

Chase Edmunds enjoys two rare tender moments on Day 3—with Kim Bauer (above) and when he was reunited with his then-infant daughter, Angela (below).

CAPTURED

Salazar gang thugs captured Edmunds on Day 3 after he followed Jack Bauer to Mexico following the Ramon Salazar prison break. He didn't know Bauer was working undercover to re-infiltrate the Salazar gang, and for a time, it appeared the mistake would cost his life. The Salazars used Edmunds to test Bauer's loyalty, and the result was excruciating torture for Edmunds. Eventually, with help from Claudia Salazar, Edmunds escaped.

Claudia aids Chase Edmunds in a desperate attempt to get her family away from the Salazars. Her plan worked, as she, Chase, her father and brother narrowly escaped. But tragically, Claudia was killed in the effort.

CTU AGENTS

CTU requires agents with a wide range of skills who are able to perform a variety of duties under pressure. They are frequently called upon to multi-task in order to fufill a mission's requirements. For instance, on Day 3, Gael Ortega was undercover posing as an analyst, but actually was a seasoned field operative with a CIA background. The agency employs field agents, analysts, and TAC unit members, plus doctors, interrogation experts, pilots, IT staff, and people in many other categories. Regardless of their specialty, all CTU personnel are certified counter-terrorist agents, and therefore must have basic weapons, martial arts, and computer training. However, field agents—who normally report to the Director of Field Operations—have more extensive weapons and tactical training, while data analysts—who typically report to the Chief of Staff—are primarily focused on computer systems and analysis training.

Deep Undercover

CIA agent, Gael Ortega, began Day 3 deep undercover, posing as a data analyst posing as a mole. He came to CTU prior to Day 3, and joined Jack Bauer and Tony Almeida's operation to infiltrate the Salazar drug cartel. Ortega's job was to be Hector Salazar's mole at CTU—to misdirect the agency's investigation of the Cordilla Virus plot while Bauer broke Ramon Salazar out of jail. Ortega was caught during an accidental encounter with Kim Bauer, but accepted torture rather than divulge the plan until he got Bauer's signal that he was safely inside.

At 3:58 a.m. on Day 3, Gael Ortega discovers the virus detonator under the Chandler Plaza Hotel's main ventilator fan.

Ortega attempted to disarm the detonator, but the device goes off, and the weaponized vapor sprays into his face.

FATAL ENCOUNTER

After having his status cleared up by Tony Almeida, Gael Ortega later joined Michelle Dessler's team at the Chandler Plaza Hotel. The agents rushed into the hotel without HAZMAT suits in a desperate race to find the Cordilla Virus canister which had been placed there by one of Stephen Saunders' confederates. It was Ortega who discovered the device placed in the hotel's ventilation system and attempted to disarm it, but hesitated just slightly, and it detonated. Ortega inhaled the weaponized virus, and rapidly became sick as the virus took hold. After suffering the horrible of the effects of the virus, Ortega died, having declined the chance to commit suicide due to his Catholic faith.

TOM BAKER

Tom Baker has served stints as Director of Field Operations for CTU. Baker frequently worked with Jack Bauer—he helped Bauer rescue Kate Warner and capture Syed Ali on Day 2, and capture Stephen Saunders on Day 3.

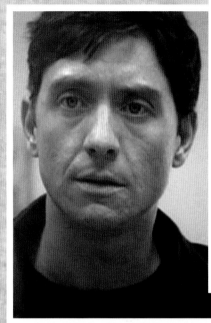

RONNIE LOBELL

Lobell was named Director of Field Operations by Erin Driscoll after she fired Jack Bauer following Day 3, and was still in charge of field ops on Day 4, when he joined Bauer to trail terrorist Kalil Hasan. They disagreed about whether to arrest Hasan or follow him, and Lobell handcuffed Bauer while he went after Hasan. The terrorist, unfortunately, killed Lobell, but with his last breath, the agent tossed his keys to Bauer so that Bauer could pursue Hasan.

HOWARD BERN

Bern was part of Jack Bauer's assault team that invaded the Chinese Consulate on Day 4. Chinese security agents identified him off a surveillance tape, and despite CTU's attempts to make Bern disappear, he was abducted and tortured by the Chinese. They forced details from him about CTU's attack on the consulate, shredding the government's cover story about the incident, and setting up their operation to capture Jack Bauer in retaliation.

LEE CASTLE

Castle was a field operative on Day 4 who butted heads with Tony Almeida after Almeida's return to CTU, especially when Almeida stopped Castle from physically abusing Dina Araz at one point. Castle then participated in a raid at a nightclub designed to capture Habib Marwan, and later joined Almeida in hunting for the killer Mandy. But she got the drop on Castle and killed him before taking Almeida hostage.

TED PAULSON

Paulson was a veteran field agent assigned to provide security for Teri and Kim Bauer at a CTU safe house on Day 1. Paulson was alone in the house with Jack Bauer's wife and daughter when thugs working for the Drazens arrived. He hid Teri and Kim, and managed to kill one of the attackers before being shot himself. He later died in the hospital, but his brave actions gave Kim and Teri the opportunity to escape.

TEDDY HANLIN

Jack Bauer had history with Hanlin before they worked together on Day 1. Years earlier, Bauer had arrested Hanlin's partner in the corruption probe that had ended Christopher Henderson's CTU career. On Day 1 Hanlin was Bauer's backup as he met a man linked to Alexis Drazen. Hanlin prematurely shot the suspect, causing him to fall to his death. Bauer was furious with Hanlin and never worked with him again.

RICK BURKE

Some time after Day 4, Burke became CTU's expert in extreme interrogation techniques. He used truth drugs on Christopher Henderson on Day 5, until Tony Almeida knocked him out—Burke was unconscious when Henderson killed Almeida and escaped. On Day 6, Burke helped Jack interrogate Graem Bauer, but he objected when Jack tried to push him into using potentially deadly amounts of hyoscine-pentothal on his brother.

ERIC RICHARDS

Going into Day 3, through Day 4, Richards served as CTU's lead interrogator. On Day 3, he helped interrogate Gael Ortega, when Ortega was thought to be a mole, and that same day, he used truth drugs on Nina Myers—he was the agent inserting a needle into her neck, in fact, when Myers intentionally caused the needle to nick an artery. On Day 4, Richards also interrogated Richard Heller and Sarah Gavin.

DR. MARC BESSON

Besson was CTU's chief medical officer going into Day 4, through to the end of Day 5. A trained surgeon, he was operating on Paul Raines on Day 4, when Jack Bauer forced him to stop in favor of saving the life of Chinese scientist Lee Jong. Besson was also in charge of the CTU medical clinic on Day 5, supervising Tony Almeida's care. Almeida knocked him out when he went after Christopher Henderson.

HARRY SWINTON

Swinton was a CTU security guard responsible for confining Lynn McGill to Holding Room 4 on Day 5, leaving them trapped together during the Sentox nerve gas attack. Since Holding Room 4 was adjacent to the building's ventilation system controls, McGill's mission to vent the gas from the building meant certain death for both men. Swinton briefly spoke to his daughter first, McGill then opened the door, and they were both dead minutes later.

CTU TAC TEAM

CTU's assault squad is commonly called the Tactical (TAC) team. TAC units generally consist of highly trained former military and/or law enforcement officers, often with SWAT or Special Forces backgrounds. They are typically utilized for hostage rescues, surprise assaults at suspected terrorist locations, and firefights. TAC methods and equipment are largely derived from classic SWAT and military protocols. Unlike military units, however, they routinely operate in urban areas, and often have to collaborate with CTU field agents and other law enforcement agencies. CTU's Director of Field Operations normally commands TAC units. He is empowered to make all tactical decisions under fire, but will consult with the agent in charge of particular missions when circumstances permit. Members are trained experts in the use of explosives, firearms, and hand-to-hand combat.

QUICK STRIKE

Director of Field Operations Curtis Manning (left) commanded the TAC unit that assaulted the Wallace home early on Day 6, rescuing Scott Wallace as CTU furiously chased leads about nuclear weapons in the possession of Abu Fayed. The operation went off without a hitch, but Manning had a fatal encounter a few minutes later.

SWAT

TAC teams evolved from law enforcement's SWAT (Special Weapons and Tactics) concept. The Los Angeles Police Department (LAPD) is generally credited with activating the first SWAT unit in the late 1960s, and that unit gained national prominence in 1974 when it engaged Symbionese Liberation Army members in a bloody shootout. Typically, many SWAT officers are ex-military, and that is certainly true of CTU's TAC leaders. Recent CTU Field Operation director Mike Doyle and former directors Jack Bauer, Curtis Manning, and Tom Baker all had extensive military experience, and Bauer (LAPD) and Manning (Boston PD) both are also SWAT veterans.

Telescoping buttstock (rear grip area) in non-retracted mode

Aimpoint red dot sighting system

PentagonLight tactical laser light system

Knights Armament Modular Rail interface system—useful for attaching lights, lasers, grips, and other add-on devices

Standard 14-inch M4 barrel with flash hiders

Tango Down forward hand grip— bottom cap is removable for storage of spare batteries and other peripherals

Wilderness Giles 3-point tactical sling

Ejection port for safe expulsion of spent rounds, with dust cover flap

The M4's magazine—the storage and feeding device for ammunition cartridges stored within

M4 CARBINE

CTU's primary assault rifle is the M4 Carbine—a descendent of the legendary M16. The M4 is shorter and lighter than the M16, features a telescoping stock, and fires in semi-automatic or automatic modes. Its flexibility has long made M4 a preferred special forces weapon, and CTU is no exception.

Lightweight Kevlar composite,
Level IIIA ballistic helmet

Shatterproof polycarbonate
protective goggles

CTU emblem patch, standard
on all CTU-issued coveralls

Safariland tactical, molded
plastic leg holster with secure
top strap, for use with a wide
range of combat pistols

READY FOR ACTION

In the field, the exact equipment package used by
TAC Team members depends on the team member's
specialty and assignment, but members are always
equipped with the latest body armor technology and
weaponry. Uniforms typically include fire-resistant
coveralls, body armor vest, heat and fire-resistant gloves,
protective eye goggles, Kevlar helmet, and combat
boots. TAC team members typically carry a
sidearm, carbine or submachine gun, tear gas,
stun grenades, tasers, flashlight, and flex
cuffs for subduing suspects.

Tactical utility vest for bearing
loads, including weapon magazines,
mini radio (in shoulder pouch),
and other specialized gear

Gas mask pouch

CLOSING IN

In day 3 TAC team members
take up positions surrounding
a building in which Stephen
Saunders is trapped. The plan
fell apart, however, after Tony
Almeida intentionally repositioned
personnel to permit Saunders
to escape, as part of Almeida's
desperate ploy to rescue Michelle.

PISTOL

TAC team members, including Jack
Bauer, frequently carry the Heckler
and Koch (HK) USP Compact
pistol. The gun frame's modest
weight, due to the use of specially
molded polymers, combined with
mechanical recoil reduction
technology, make it useful for
combat and undercover work.

Classic steel-toe SWAT combat boots

CTU TECHNOLOGY

CTU SUV's normally travel with specially designed, pullout vehicle storage systems, or "gun safes," although the lockable drawers also carry other delicate equipment, depending on the mission.

Due to its location in sprawling Los Angeles, and a constant need to transport agents and equipment around the city, the Los Angeles Domestic Unit of CTU requires a large vehicle fleet. The primary mode of transportation for field agents is the Sports Utility Vehicle (SUV), and currently, CTU LA utilizes specially configured, stretched versions of black 2007 Ford Expedition SUVs, seating up to seven agents. Among the vehicle modifications for CTU's needs are front grille and windshield police lights, rear cab floodlights, satellite communication equipment, digital media stations, and a proprietary gun safe to transport a wide range of weapons and equipment, which slides smoothly out of the rear cab. CTU also maintains a range of Dodge Sprinter tactical vans for surveillance, Toyota Tundra pickup trucks, and Cadillac limousines for visiting dignitaries.

Luggage rails are often used as hand grips by agents riding on the vehicle's exterior in emergency situations

Emergency strobe lights

Ultra-bright, complex surface halogen headlights

In emergencies agents can stand on ledge when riding on outside of moving vehicle

Police-style LED strobe grille lights

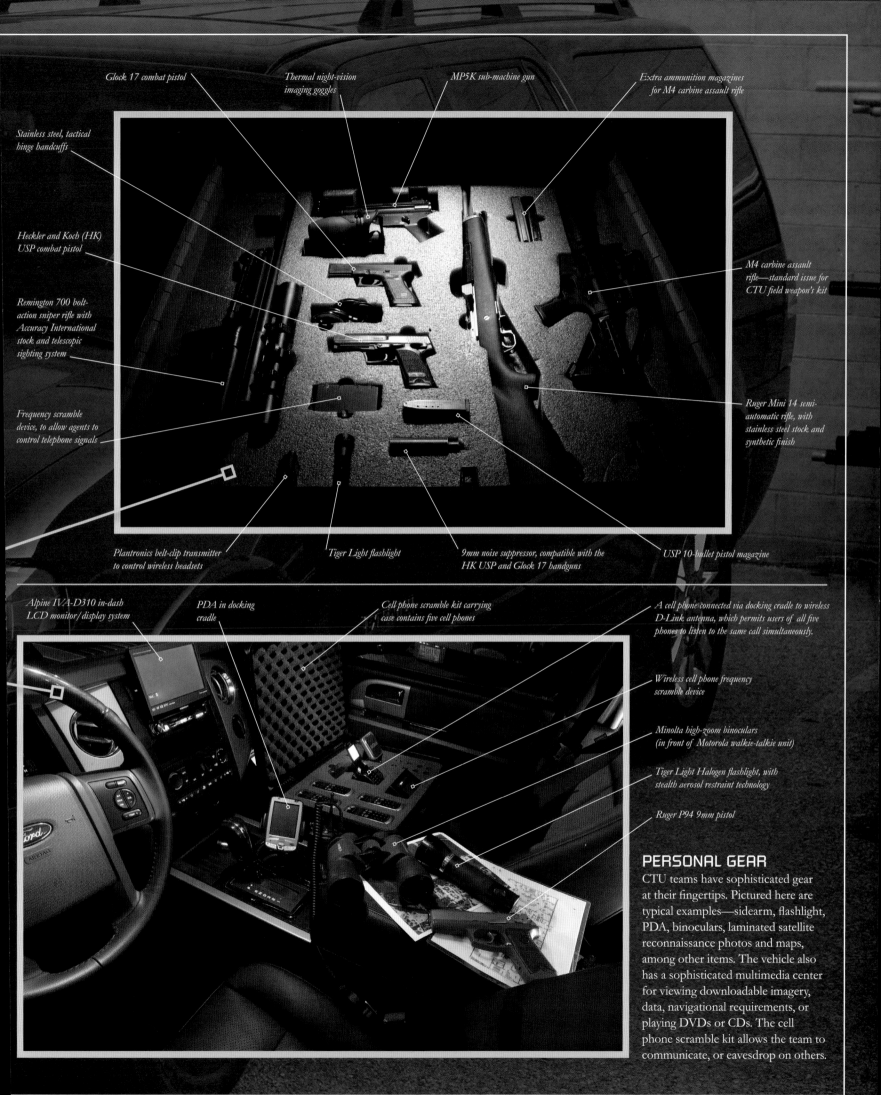

Glock 17 combat pistol

Thermal night-vision imaging goggles

MP5K sub-machine gun

Extra ammunition magazines for M4 carbine assault rifle

Stainless steel, tactical hinge handcuffs

Heckler and Koch (HK) USP combat pistol

M4 carbine assault rifle—standard issue for CTU field weapon's kit

Remington 700 bolt-action sniper rifle with Accuracy International stock and telescopic sighting system

Frequency scramble device, to allow agents to control telephone signals

Ruger Mini 14 semi-automatic rifle, with stainless steel stock and synthetic finish

Plantronics belt-clip transmitter to control wireless headsets

Tiger Light flashlight

9mm noise suppressor, compatible with the HK USP and Glock 17 handguns

USP 10-bullet pistol magazine

Alpine IVA-D310 in-dash LCD monitor/display system

PDA in docking cradle

Cell phone scramble kit carrying case contains five cell phones

A cell phone connected via docking cradle to wireless D-Link antenna, which permits users of all five phones to listen to the same call simultaneously.

Wireless cell phone frequency scramble device

Minolta high-zoom binoculars (in front of Motorola walkie-talkie unit)

Tiger Light Halogen flashlight, with stealth aerosol restraint technology

Ruger P94 9mm pistol

PERSONAL GEAR

CTU teams have sophisticated gear at their fingertips. Pictured here are typical examples—sidearm, flashlight, PDA, binoculars, laminated satellite reconnaissance photos and maps, among other items. The vehicle also has a sophisticated multimedia center for viewing downloadable imagery, data, navigational requirements, or playing DVDs or CDs. The cell phone scramble kit allows the team to communicate, or eavesdrop on others.

CTU TECHNOLOGY

CTU has a sophisticated technology infrastructure and staff to design and build proprietary tools and weapons to use inside CTU and in the field, and also to procure the most advanced off-shelf technology available and adapt that equipment to the specific needs of missions. Through the Federal government, the agency also maintains private contracts with manufacturers of high-end technology to produce proprietary versions of commercially available products. For example, CTU agents typically use commercially available cell phones, but with uniquely designed GPS locator chips inside, as well as specially encrypted data cards to make them compatible with sensitive government security protocols. Particularly in the categories of communications, interrogation, and observation technologies, CTU leads the way inside the government in terms of innovating technology breakthroughs that often have wider applications for other agencies.

ACCESS CONTROL

For access into sensitive areas, CTU relies on the HID bioCLASS "smart card" identification system. Essentially, it can demand up to three levels of identification before allowing entrance to a secure area: swiping an encrypted ID card, a keypad for inputting a unique PIN number, and a biometric touchpad scanner for identifying fingerprints.

TELLING THE TRUTH

CTU uses a physiological monitoring polygraph system during interrogations to judge if prisoners are telling the truth. When a suspect wears the wrist-cuffs, CTU can monitor heart rate, respiratory system, pulse, body temperature, and other vital signs to analyze their intent during questioning. The blue switching hub transfers data into black digital "filter boxes," where each vital sign is isolated and fed into a sophisticated computer system for real-time analysis.

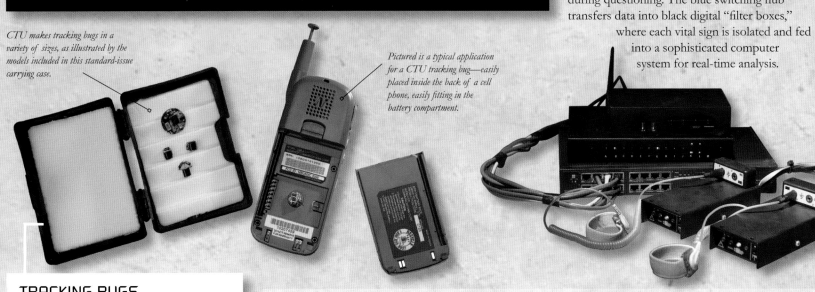

CTU makes tracking bugs in a variety of sizes, as illustrated by the models included in this standard-issue carrying case.

Pictured is a typical application for a CTU tracking bug—easily placed inside the back of a cell phone, easily fitting in the battery compartment.

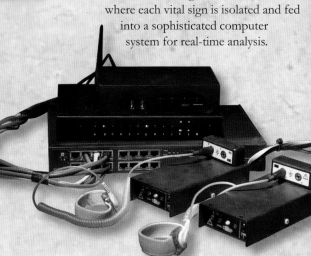

TRACKING BUGS

CTU uses miniature tracking bugs of different sizes to track locations of suspects and agents. The bugs send out a unique radio frequency at a specific bandwidth, and CTU monitoring stations track that frequency's direction and altitude. Here, one of the bugs is shown planted inside a cell phone, but the devices can be placed in various locations.

COM UNITS

CTU commonly uses wireless micro-transmitters, nicknamed "earwigs," form-fitted for the ears of specific field agents, to communicate during undercover work. Com units allow agents to hear communications when it is not feasible to use a cell phone, radio, or walkie-talkie. If two-way communication is required, earwigs can be used in combination with an ultra-tiny "throat mic."

MOBILE RECORDING

CTU agents often carry a mobile video monitoring system like this one into the field. The system is designed to allow agents to install Web-style video cameras in inconspicuous places, and monitor them from another location close by, or their vehicle, using wireless technology. The kit gives CTU a simple way to set up instant video reconnaissance.

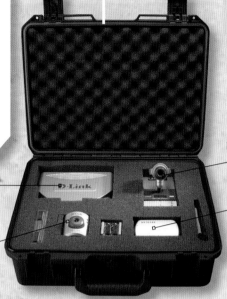

MOBILE VIEWING

CTU field teams frequently use this kind of kit to view imagery transmitted by a mobile observation system. Typically, a 4¼-quarter-inch LCD monitor, a couple of control units to operate cameras from afar, and additional circuit boards are part of the field viewing package.

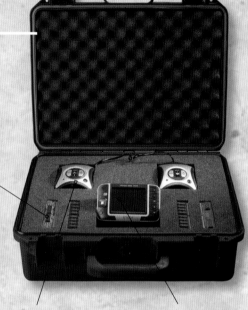

Lynksys/Cisco Wireless G 2.4GHz Internet camera

D-Link wireless broadband video phone adapter hub

Netgear video hub

D-Link DCS-900W 2.4GHz wireless Internet camera

Removable, interchangeable circuit boards, depending on the broadcast frequency being used.

RECORDING INTERROGATIONS

When CTU interrogates suspects in the field, agents document it whenever possible—as on Day 6 with Graem Bauer. For this purpose, they carry a video recording package that includes up to four Panasonic VDR-D300 DVD camcorders to permanently record interrogations to digital media. But the package also features a Logitech Internet camera to stream imagery in real-time to CTU.

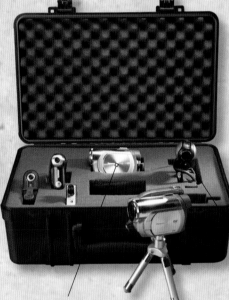

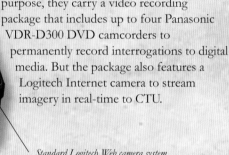

Standard Logitech Web camera system for easy streaming with any conventional broadband connection.

Panasonic VDR-D300 DVD camcorders with high-resolution, 3-CCD sensor and onboard DVD recorder for simple file transfer.

Kit features two router antenna control devices to remotely control camera focus, pan, and tilt.

iRiver quarter-inch LCD monitor, adapted from iRiver portable media center viewing technology.

ENEMY TECHNOLOGY

Terrorists are not without their own technological capabilities, and the phone scrambler device exemplifies that. Operating under the radar, they can't rely on sophisticated networks like CTU does, but the scrambler allows them to remotely encrypt communications between cell phones. During Day 6, Abu Fayed and his confederates used a device similar to the one pictured here.

TORTURE KIT

Agent Rick Burke's so-called "torture kit" is used by CTU in extreme circumstances to extract information from suspects like Christopher Henderson and Graem Bauer, among others. The kit consists of medical syringes and various bottles of intravenously delivered "truth drugs," particularly Hyoscine-Pentothal.

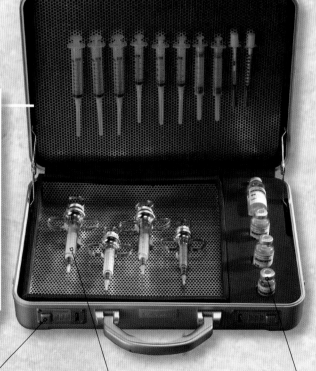

Vanguard stainless steel medical carrying case

Standard medical syringes

Four bottles of Hyoscine-Pentothal "truth drug" used for interrogating suspects.

CTU'S ARSENAL

The Los Angeles Domestic Unit of CTU has an on-site armory that houses an arsenal of sophisticated military and law-enforcement weaponry. Agents normally carry a sidearm and most favor one of three 9mm pistols—a Glock 19 semi-automatic pistol, a Heckler and Koch (HK) USP Compact, or a Sig Sauer P226 Luger. In addition, agents usually carry a knife and stun gun. TAC unit equipment packages include M4 carbine assault rifles, Ruger Mini 14 semi-automatic assault rifles, sniper rifles, and various machine guns in different configurations. A variety of more specialized weaponry, ranging from stun grenades to shoulder-mounted missile launchers, can be incorporated into weapon packages for particular missions, along with a wide range of explosives.

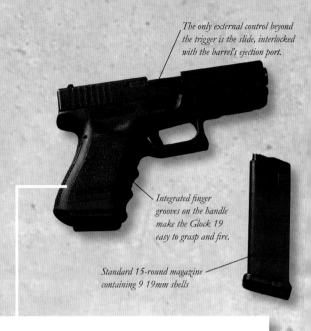

The only external control beyond the trigger is the slide, interlocked with the barrel's ejection port.

Integrated finger grooves on the handle make the Glock 19 easy to grasp and fire.

Standard 15-round magazine containing 9 19mm shells

GLOCK 19
The Glock 19 semi-automatic pistol is popular with many CTU agents, including Mike Doyle—Curtis Manning's replacement as Director of Field Operations on Day 6. The Glock 19 is a mid-size semi-automatic weapon, configured here with a 15-round magazine. It is popular in the world of law enforcement.

Adjustable rear iron diopter sight

Front post iron diopter sight

Forward handle for stability firing around corners

S-E-F selector switch to choose firing mode— safe (S), single-shot (E), or full-auto (F).

30-round detachable box magazine holds 30 rounds per clip

H&K MP5K
The Heckler & Koch MP5K is a compact, fully automatic machine gun. Its modest weight allows agents to easily transport and conceal major firepower in short-range situations. It also offers great flexibility with multiple firing modes.

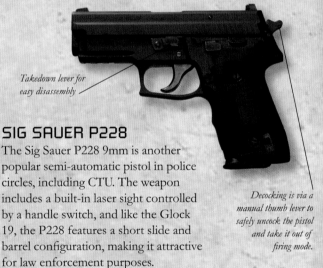

Takedown lever for easy disassembly

SIG SAUER P228
The Sig Sauer P228 9mm is another popular semi-automatic pistol in police circles, including CTU. The weapon includes a built-in laser sight controlled by a handle switch, and like the Glock 19, the P228 features a short slide and barrel configuration, making it attractive for law enforcement purposes.

Decocking is via a manual thumb lever to safely uncock the pistol and take it out of firing mode.

Electrodes distribute a powerful electrical charge transferred from capacitors inside the circuitry

Designs vary on electro-shock weapons. This unit is molded at an angle for a right-handed user.

STUN GUNS
These CTU-issue stun guns are Stun Master models, ranging from 200,000 to 300,000 volts. They fire electrical charges into the nervous system, rather than causing massive pain. But CTU has been known to increase voltage to make them lethal devices.

The lightweight carbon-fiber stock has a texture similar to molded plastic.

Adjustable rear iron sight

Shoulder strap

Extended magazine release for .223 Remington cartridges

RUGER MINI 14

The Ruger Mini-14 semiautomatic rifle is useful for CTU field teams because it is an ultra lightweight gun. Built with a light carbon-fiber stock, the rifle offers heavy firepower in the form of a .223 Remington cartridge. It was originally designed for hunting, but has proven popular with law enforcement in recent years.

POCKET BLADES

Most CTU field agents carry a knife, usually a version of a MicroTech HALO automatic switchblade. As shown here, various models are part of CTU's kit, but all are spring-loaded, stainless steel knives—some spring straight from the handle, and some flip open.

Appears to be an ordinary clipboard

WEAPONS OF TERROR

Modern terrorists are well financed and trained, and have ample access to weapons-grade materials, such as C4 explosives. Despite their pursuit of weapons of mass destruction, they regularly do significant damage with simpler weapons, such as suicide bomb vests and other conventional explosives.

CLIPBOARD BOMB

At 4:54 p.m. on Day 5, Christopher Henderson detonated a bomb inside a metal clipboard to kill Jack Bauer at Omicron International. It was a sophisticated device, filled with 12 ounces of C4. It failed to kill Bauer because he hid in a crawlspace in the floor.

A timer unit wired to C4 explosive detonated the bomb after a wireless signal from Henderson

Concealed explosive device

DAY 5 CRISIS

At 9:45 a.m. on Day 5, CTU remotely detonated a bomb vest like this one, worn by terrorists during the Ontario Airport crisis. The vests had flaws that allowed them to be detonated using a wireless code, so CTU obtained the code, and Jack Bauer set one off to save Derek Huxley.

Vest locking mechanism—once locked onto the terrorist and the number dials turned, it is impossible to open, in the event of a change of heart.

DAY 6 BOMBER

A bomb vest was worn early on Day 6 by a follower of Abu Fayed's named Nasir. He intended to detonate a suicide bomb on the Los Angeles subway. As Nasir reached to press the detonator, Jack Bauer managed to push him out of the car before the vest exploded.

Box had a silver switch for manually detonating the bomb vest.

Vest held nine blocks of C4 explosive—five in the front and four in the back.

Handheld button detonator for suicide vest, wired directly to detonation box and C4 blocks

Seven blocks of C4 plastic explosive, make the vest extremely powerful.

AERIAL DYNAMICS

With speed usually of the essence, CTU relies heavily on helicopters to help agents circumvent the city's massive traffic web while maneuvering between locations. As a result, CTU maintains a fleet of Bell 206 JetRanger helicopters as general transport vehicles to quickly move agents around the LA Metropolitan area. CTU also has access to a wide range of other air vehicles that it either operates itself or borrows from other agencies. For instance, the agency periodically uses Eurocopter AS350B A-Star helicopters for special ops stealth missions, and the Bell 212 Twin Huey for transporting large teams for major assaults. CTU also has access to airplanes when necessary, such as Gulfstream corporate jets, to ferry dignitaries. When major aerial firepower is needed, however, CTU normally relies on military assistance.

SUICIDE MISSION

On Day 2, to swiftly remove a nuclear device from Norton Airfield, Jack Bauer had only a small, private plane available—a Cessna 208 Caravan. He flew it to a remote, unpopulated area over the Mojave Desert, where the dying George Mason insisted on finishing the suicide mission, while Bauer parachuted to safety.

SHOOTDOWN

On Day 5, Bauer hijacked a private jet in pursuit of the audio recording incriminating President Logan, carried by the plane's co-pilot. President Logan ordered the Navy to scramble F/A-18 Hornet fighter jets, including the one pictured here, to shoot the plane down. Admiral Kirkland at the Point Mugu Command Center and the F/A-18 pilot both resisted Logan's demand when it became clear the plane was not a threat, and the attack was eventually aborted.

DELICATE CARGO

A Lockheed C-130 Hercules military transport plane prepares to deposit highly sensitive cargo at Ellis Airfield at 6:08 a.m. on Day 6—Jack Bauer, returned after 18 months in a Chinese military prison. Bauer was escorted by Chinese security official Cheng Zhi, who tortured him during his captivity, in this transport plane. But the C-130 is widely used by many nations for military tactical purposes, including the U.S.. It was originally designed as an assault transport vehicle, but is used for all sorts of different missions, ranging from cargo transport, to surveillance, and special ops.

The C-130 is a four-engine turboprop aircraft that has been in production for over 50 years as a standard military transport plane. Recently its use has been expanded for search-and-rescue, aerial refueling, firefighting, and humanitarian missions.

STEALTH FIGHTER

On Day 4, one of the most audacious terror acts in recent history occurred when disgraced former Air Force officer Mitch Anderson betrayed his country, stole an F-117A Nighthawk Stealth fighter, and used it to shoot down Air Force One. The jet was later fired on and destroyed by Air Force fighters, but not until after Anderson carried out his attack. That's because the plane, once airborne, was extremely difficult to locate due to its specific design to avoid radar detection. The F-117A, however, is an older stealth design, and is currently being phased out of use by the Air Force, in favor of the newer F-17 Raptor.

The Bauer's scrambled into the helicopter at 12:57 p.m., and less than five minutes later, they returned to CTU. Since the BellRanger can travel up to 139 mph, with proper clearance on a priority mission, it can usually ferry people between CTU and most locations in the greater Los Angeles area within minutes.

RESCUE VEHICLE

At 12:57 p.m. on Day 1, a Bell 206 JetRanger airlifts Teri, Kim, and Jack Bauer from Ira Gaines' compound after Jack Bauer rescued his family. As soon as Bauer called in from the location, CTU dispatched the helicopter. It first helped drive off Gaines' men, and then conducted the rescue operation.

QUICK TRANSPORT

Curtis Manning meets Bauer's helicopter at Jacob Rossler's building at 1:22 p.m. on Day 5. Rossler was suspected of aiding Ivan Erwich's plan to detonate nerve gas canisters. CTU had only minutes to take him down, and the ability of the Bell 206 JetRanger helicopter to swiftly transport Bauer to the location was crucial.

The Bell 206 JetRanger is CTU's primary aerial transport vehicle in and around Los Angeles, as its use on Day 5 illustrates. The JetRanger is a two-bladed, turbine-powered helicopter with a conventional two-bladed tail rotor and hydraulic flight controls. It is heavily used by United States Armed Forces.

GOVERNMENT

During a crisis, CTU often reports directly to officials at the highest levels of the U.S. government, including the President of the United States. At such times, fearless leadership is required to make heart-wrenching and morally troubling decisions that frequently decide who lives and who dies. Over the years, officials within the administrations of David Palmer, Charles Logan, and Wayne Palmer have often risen to this challenge—but not always. Sadly, bad judgment, misguided patriotism, fear, corruption, cowardice, and other personal failings have all been found lurking in the shadows of power.

DAVID PALMER

David Palmer's life represents an American success story wrapped in a Shakespearian tragedy. A student-athlete at Georgetown University, Palmer went to law school, married Sherry, had two children, worked as a lawyer, and served in the Maryland State Legislature and both houses of Congress before running for president. During the California Primary on Day 1, the Drazen terror plot—which included two assassination attempts—and a family scandal almost destroyed him, but in the end, Palmer did capture the presidency. The price was his marriage, as Sherry's political maneuvering proved intolerable. For the next four years, especially during Days 2 and 3, his administration was rocked by scandals, a wave of terror plots, his temporary removal from office, and an assassination attempt, which he barely survived on Day 2. After Sherry's violent death on Day 3, Palmer decided not to seek re-election. On Day 4, former President Palmer advised acting President Logan during a major crisis, but then, early on Day 5, he was murdered.

SUPER TUESDAY

For David Palmer, Day 1 had another name—Super Tuesday. That term generally refers to a cluster of U.S. political primaries that take place on the same day, usually in early March. These often play a major role in deciding who will be nominated to run for president from one, or both, major American political parties. Day 1 took place during Super Tuesday, and despite the day's turbulent events, Palmer's reputation and his emotional speech to the nation allowed him to sweep all 11 primaries, including the biggest prize of them all—California. After capturing the Democratic nomination, Palmer wrestled the presidency from the incumbent Harold Barnes.

FAMILY MEETING

As primary voters head to the polls on Day 1, David Palmer asks his family to support his decision to go public about a personal scandal. Seven years earlier, his son, Keith, had been involved in the death of a man who had raped his sister, Nicole. For most of Day 1 Sherry Palmer had struggled to keep that information firstly from her husband and later from the public. Against his wife's wishes, Palmer decided to come clean at a press conference, continuing the unraveling of their marriage.

Palmer Family Tree

President Wayne Palmer (brother)

Attorney Sandra Palmer (sister)

President David Palmer

Sherry Palmer (former wife)

Keith Palmer (son)

Nicole Palmer (daughter)

INTERLUDE

As Day 2 gets underway, President David Palmer enjoys one of the final peaceful moments of his tumultuous presidency while fishing with his son at Oregon's Lake Oswego. Moments later, he would learn about a nuclear terror threat against the United States and rush to a secure bunker at the nearby Northwest Regional Operations Complex. Before the day was over, he would resist pressure to start a major war, be temporarily removed from power, and be struck down in an assassination attempt.

DAVID PALMER

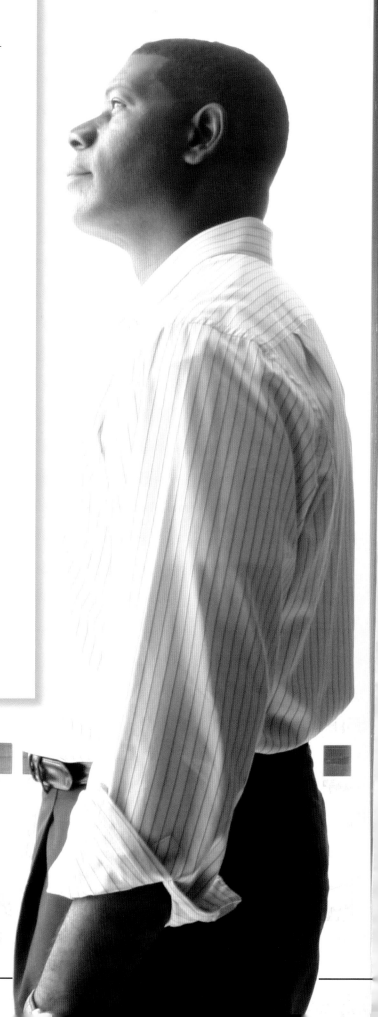

At 7:02 a.m. on Day 5, a melancholy former president David Palmer contemplates his life while writing his memoirs at his brother Wayne's high-rise apartment overlooking Los Angeles. Seconds later, he was dead. A high-powered rifle blast through the window sliced through Palmer's neck, killing him instantly. The assassination—carried out by a sniper named Haas, on orders from Christopher Henderson, and designed to implicate Jack Bauer—was part of a violent conspiracy. Although Palmer died, he proved to be a key player in unraveling that conspiracy. He was killed because he had discovered evidence about the impending Sentox nerve gas attacks, and planned to bring that evidence to First Lady, Martha Logan. Clues he left behind in his manuscript were discovered by Wayne Palmer and Jack Bauer and proved crucial to stopping the plot.

Moments before his assassination David Palmer shares a tender moment with his brother, Wayne. As Day 5 began, Wayne, David's longtime closest adviser, sensed that his brother was troubled about something. David Palmer was shot before he could confide in Wayne about the Sentox nerve gas plot, and died helplessly in his brother's arms. Wayne later helped Jack Bauer solve the plot and get that information to the authorities, despite an attempt on his own life.

PRESIDENTIAL ASSASSINATIONS

David Palmer was the first former president to be assassinated. In fact, only one other former president faced a murder attempt—Theodore Roosevelt in 1912. Roosevelt left office in 1909, but was running again in 1912 when he was shot during a campaign stop in Milwaukee. The bullet glanced off the manuscript of Roosevelt's speech in his pocket before lodging in his chest. The wound was not deep, and he survived, although he lost his presidential bid. The only sitting presidents to be killed by assassins were Abraham Lincoln, James Garfield, William McKinley, and John F. Kennedy. Presidents Andrew Jackson, Franklin Roosevelt (as President-elect), Harry S. Truman, Gerald Ford (twice), and Ronald Reagan all survived assassination attempts.

RELIEVED OF COMMAND

Vice President Jim Prescott takes the reigns of power on Day 2 after masterminding the removal of David Palmer from office. Prescott took over after Palmer refused to launch military action while CTU investigated the nuclear threat. Prescott claimed Palmer was unnerved by the day's pressure and unfit to command. Palmer was later vindicated when Jack Bauer proved Peter Kingsley had manufactured the crisis, and Prescott stepped aside. A short time later, Prescott again became Acting President when

25TH AMENDMENT

The device used to remove David Palmer from office in favor of Vice President Jim Prescott on Day 2 was the fourth clause of the 25th Amendment to the Constitution. Congress passed the amendment in 1965 to codify the line of succession and procedures in the event the president becomes incapacitated and unable to perform his duties. It states that when the Vice President and a majority of the Cabinet determines the president is unfit to serve, he can be removed and temporarily replaced by the Vice President.

UNEASY ALLIANCE

David Palmer reluctantly accepts help from ex-wife Sherry on Day 2, although he is unsure of her true agenda. Sherry offered the President information on a conspiracy within the administration, and Palmer eventually gave in after she appeared to implicate NSA head Roger Stanton in the plot. It turned out that Sherry and Stanton were both cooperating with Peter Kingsley in order to bring down Palmer's presidency. Sherry's motive was revenge against Palmer—for ending their marriage and denying her the chance to be First Lady.

RE-ELECTION DERAILED

As part of his reelection campaign on Day 3, David Palmer debates with his Republican opponent, Senator John Keeler. During the debate, Palmer grappled with an unneeded complication when Keeler alleged that Palmer's personal physician and also romantic partner, Dr. Anne Packard, had engaged in financial improprieties with her former husband at a pharmaceutical company. The charge was false, but Packard's former husband, Ted, committed suicide after giving her evidence that cleared them. The incident caused Packard to end her relationship with the President. Keeler won the election when Palmer withdrew from the race after Day 3.

PRESIDENTIAL ADVISER

On Day 4, former President David Palmer was summoned to the White House to advise President Charles Logan on the stolen nuclear warhead crisis, and Logan permitted Palmer to make command decisions. Among his choices, Palmer authorized Jack Bauer's covert mission at the Chinese Consulate in Los Angeles and urged Logan to pardon the mysterious assassin known as Mandy—the same woman who tried to kill him on Day 2—in order to secure Habib Marwan's location. But his biggest contribution involved saving Jack Bauer's life by warning him of a plot to kill him, leading Bauer to fake his death and go into hiding.

SHERRY PALMER

Sherry Palmer grew up with David Palmer, married him, and gave him two children while steadfastly supporting his career. During that time, though, she harbored burning ambitions of her own—ambitions that ended up destroying her life and Palmer's presidency. By Day 1, as her husband fought for the Democratic nomination, she began engaging in the worst kinds of political hardball. Her lack of ethics backfired that day, when on the eve of her greatest triumph—ascension to the role of First Lady—Palmer decided to divorce her. Bitter, she became embroiled in Peter Kingsley's terror conspiracy on Day 2. And then, on Day 3, she attempted to return to Palmer's inner circle with disastrous results after she inadvertently caused Alan Milliken's death, and manipulated one person too many when Julia Milliken murdered her.

Despite ending their marriage, David Palmer twice let Sherry back into his life on Days 2 and 3, with severe consequences both times. Still, to the bitter end, Sherry claimed to still love and want to help Palmer, even while taking actions to destroy his presidency.

FACT FILE

STATUS: Deceased

MARITAL STATUS:
Divorced from David Palmer at time of death

CHILDREN:
Keith Palmer and Nicole Palmer

EDUCATION:
Bachelor of Arts, Sociology, Georgetown
University

POLITICAL EXPERIENCE:
• President, Congressional Spouses Club
• Appointee to USO World Board
• Fundraising Chairwoman, Congressional
  Wives for Human Rights
• Chairman of the Board, Maryland Hunger Fund

DECEITFUL

Sherry Palmer resented David Palmer's decision to distance himself from her on Day 1, and desperate to know his plans, she convinced campaign aide Patty Brooks to spy on him. She even urged Brooks to make sexual advances toward her husband, but Palmer wanted no part of such behavior and immediately fired Brooks. The incident was the final straw for Palmer on Day 1 in terms of convincing him he needed to sever ties with Sherry. That would, of course, prove difficult, and she continued to interfere in his life and career for several more years.

FINAL CONFRONTATION

Sherry Palmer's manipulations came to a shocking end late in Day 3 when a distraught Julia Milliken, terrified she would be linked to her husband's death, killed her and then committed suicide. Julia blamed Sherry for her predicament because, earlier in the day, Sherry contributed to the death of her husband, Alan Milliken, and then convinced Julia to cover up the incident. But, as the cover-up broke down and suspicion fell on Julia, she lost control and ended the Sherry Palmer saga.

CLANDESTINE MEETING

Jack Bauer forced Sherry Palmer to meet Peter Kingsley at the Los Angeles Coliseum late on Day 2. Kingsley expected Sherry to turn over audio technician Alex Hewitt—the technical genius behind the faked Cyprus audio recording who had evidence of Kingsley's plot. But, in reality, Sherry was wearing a wire at Bauer's behest to help prove Kingsley was behind the day's events. She agreed to the meeting in the desperate hope that David Palmer would forgive her earlier role in the Kingsley affair. After Bauer's final confrontation with Kingsley, she was arrested, but Palmer eventually did have her released from custody after Day 2.

Kingsley was instantly suspicious of Sherry Palmer when they met, and ordered her killed seconds later but Jack Bauer began firing on Kingsley's men from a sniper position, allowing Sherry to escape.

Julia Milliken aims her gun at Sherry Palmer, who desperately tries to calm her. Sherry's efforts were for nothing, and second later, she was dead.

WAYNE PALMER

The trajectory of Wayne Palmer's life eerily evokes the fate of his older brother, David Palmer. Wayne was a star athlete, former marine, and successful lawyer who eventually became David's Chief of Staff. But, on Day 3, an old extra-marital affair involving Wayne caused a scandal that eventually forced David to forego re-election. Then, on Day 5, the former president was murdered—prompting Wayne to risk his own life to help bring down the Logan Administration. Months later, trying to unify the nation, he won the presidency himself, only to face a massive terror crisis on Day 6. Palmer grappled with how to respond, and his decisions led to an assassination attempt, leaving him unconscious. Miraculously, he awoke in time to halt a nuclear attack and prevent efforts to remove him from the presidency. The strain of those events was too great, however, and like David Palmer, he paid a great price: suffering a brain hemorrhage and lapsing into a coma.

COMRADES

President David Palmer (left) with his brother and then-Chief of Staff, Wayne Palmer, shown together on Day 3. Wayne was always David's closest friend and confidante, and after the dismissal of Mike Novick at the end of Day 2, David decided to turn to Wayne for counsel, naming him Chief of Staff. That decision made them the most powerful pair of brothers in the upper echelon of the Executive Branch of the Federal government since Robert Kennedy served as John F. Kennedy's Attorney General in the early 1960s.

DIRTY SECRETS

At 10:28 p.m. on Day 3, Wayne meets Julia Milliken, his former lover, to urge her to persuade her husband, Alan Milliken, to stop threats against the Palmer Administration. Milliken wanted Wayne fired after learning he and Julia had been lovers, and threatened David Palmer's legislative agenda. Julia wanted Wayne to resume their affair. When Wayne declined, she refused his request to intercede.

SANDRA PALMER

Sandra Palmer, sister of David and Wayne Palmer and a prominent civil rights attorney, was legal counselor for the Islamic-American Alliance. On Day 6 she and colleague, Walid Al-Rezani, opposed her brother's decision to put Muslims into detention centers. Sandra later made the consequential decision to have Wayne medically revived from his coma.

TAKING ACTION

At 10:53 p.m. on Day 5, Wayne Palmer finds himself forced to take action assisting Jack Bauer in rescuing Evelyn Martin's daughter from Christopher Henderson's thugs as part of an effort to avenge his brother's murder. Bauer armed the former marine and asked him to terminate a guard, although he had never shot anyone. Palmer carried through with Bauer's request and killed the man, permitting Bauer to rescue the girl.

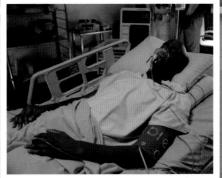

UNLIKELY DUO

On Day 6, President Wayne Palmer personally confronts a known terrorist—Hamri Al-Assad—in his White House bunker. Palmer decided to enlist Al-Assad's help in marginalizing the fanatic behind the day's attacks, Abu Fayed, by asking Al-Assad to give a speech to the Muslim world asking for an end to the bloodshed. The men were working on that speech when an assassination attempt was made against Palmer. Ironically, the man with so much blood on his hands, Al-Assad, saved Palmer's life by putting his body between Palmer and the blast. Al-Assad died instantly, while Palmer suffered severe injuries.

FACT FILE

AGE: Classified

BIRTHPLACE: Classified

MARITAL STATUS: Single

CHILDREN: None

SIBLINGS:
David (deceased) and Sandra Palmer

RELATIVES:
Keith (nephew) and Nicole Palmer (Niece); Sherry Palmer (sister-in-law, deceased)

EDUCATION:
• Juris Doctorate, Yale School of Law
• Bachelor of Arts, Political Science, Stanford University (four-year baseball scholarship)

EXPERIENCE:
• President of the United States
• Chief of Staff to the President of the United States (David Palmer)
• Milliken Enterprises, COO
• Anderson & Siebertz, Attorney at Law

MILITARY:
United States Marine Corps

COLLAPSE

Tom Lennox, Karen Hayes, and other aides rush to Wayne Palmer's side when he collapses at 11:44 p.m. on Day 6 after announcing that the terror crisis has finally passed. It was the moment of Palmer's greatest triumph as President, but the stress of pushing himself through the crisis, relying on Adrenaline shots, and not following proper medical protocols eventually caught up with him. As he spoke to the media, he collapsed from a cerebral hemorrhage, ending his presidency and putting him into a comatose state.

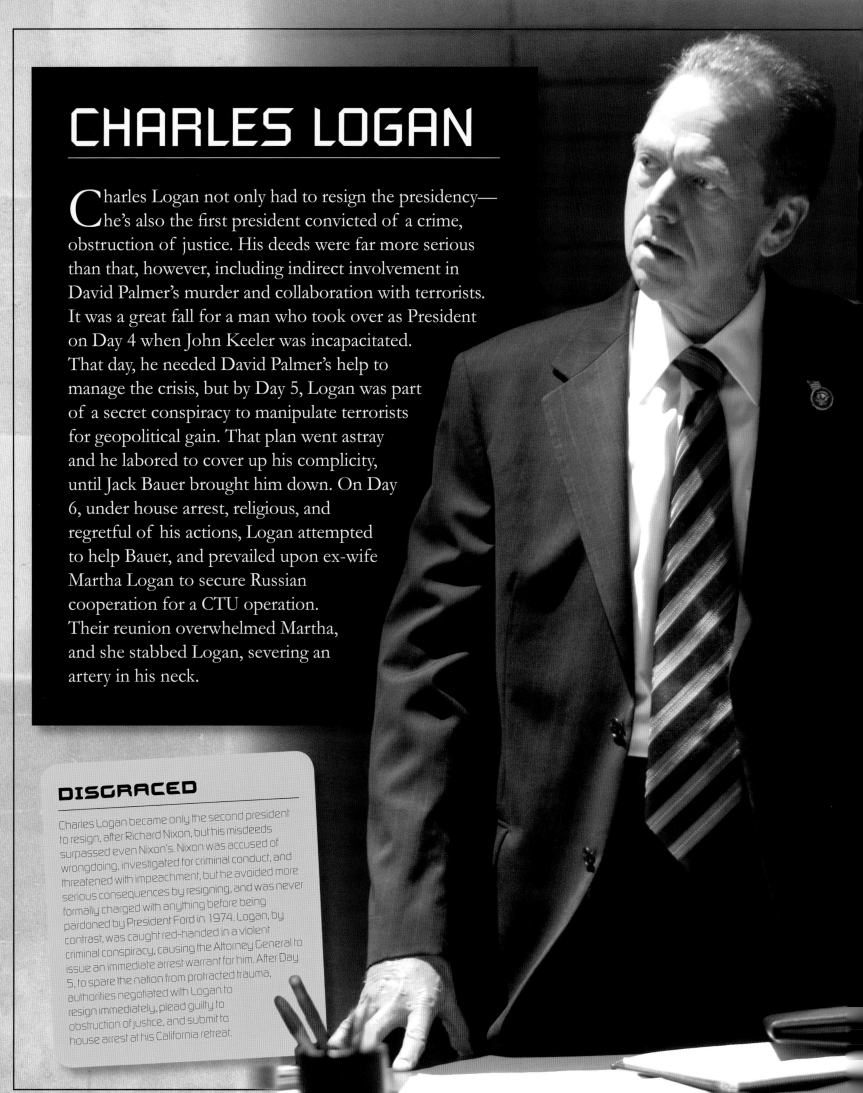

CHARLES LOGAN

Charles Logan not only had to resign the presidency—he's also the first president convicted of a crime, obstruction of justice. His deeds were far more serious than that, however, including indirect involvement in David Palmer's murder and collaboration with terrorists. It was a great fall for a man who took over as President on Day 4 when John Keeler was incapacitated. That day, he needed David Palmer's help to manage the crisis, but by Day 5, Logan was part of a secret conspiracy to manipulate terrorists for geopolitical gain. That plan went astray and he labored to cover up his complicity, until Jack Bauer brought him down. On Day 6, under house arrest, religious, and regretful of his actions, Logan attempted to help Bauer, and prevailed upon ex-wife Martha Logan to secure Russian cooperation for a CTU operation. Their reunion overwhelmed Martha, and she stabbed Logan, severing an artery in his neck.

DISGRACED

Charles Logan became only the second president to resign, after Richard Nixon, but his misdeeds surpassed even Nixon's. Nixon was accused of wrongdoing, investigated for criminal conduct, and threatened with impeachment, but he avoided more serious consequences by resigning, and was never formally charged with anything before being pardoned by President Ford in 1974. Logan, by contrast, was caught red-handed in a violent criminal conspiracy, causing the Attorney General to issue an immediate arrest warrant for him. After Day 5, to spare the nation from protracted trauma, authorities negotiated with Logan to resign immediately, plead guilty to obstruction of justice, and submit to house arrest at his California retreat.

FACT FILE

STATUS: Unknown

BIRTHPLACE: Classified

MARITAL STATUS:
Divorced from Martha Logan at time of death

CHILDREN: None

EDUCATION:
Bachelor of Arts, History, Princeton University

EXPERIENCE:

- President of the United States
- Vice President of the United States
- Republican Senator, State of California
- Lieutenant Governor of California
- California State Legislature (R-Santa Barbara)
- CEO, Western Energy Coal & Reserve
- Vice President, Western Energy, Coal & Reserve
- Director, Pacific Nuclear Energy

HONORS:
Energy CEO of the Year

DESPONDENT

Upon learning that Jack Bauer has escaped a dragnet with the recording incriminating him, Charles Logan presumes his fight to hide his criminal activity is over. He removes a .45 caliber pistol from a wooden box and seriously considers suicide. Logan delayed taking his own life long enough to visit his wife and have a drink, and before he could summon the courage, he received a call from Homeland Security official Miles Papazian at CTU, offering to destroy the recording in return for political friendship. Logan put the gun away, thus living to witness his own downfall a few hours later.

UNDER ARREST

After concluding his remarks at a memorial service for David Palmer, President Charles Logan is stunned to learn at 6:43 a.m. on Day 6 that a Federal Marshal will be taking him into custody. Logan resisted, and the Marshal pulled a transmitter device, implanted in a pen, from Logan's pocket to show him there was solid evidence behind the order. The transmitter planted on him by Jack Bauer allowed CTU to record Logan's self-incriminating comments when he bellowed at his wife a few minutes earlier. That recording was played for the Attorney General, and a warrant for Logan's arrest was immediately issued. At this moment, Logan realized his presidency was over.

CONFRONTATION

At 6:22 a.m. on Day 5, Jack Bauer threatens to shoot President Charles Logan if he does not admit to his role in the nerve gas plot. Despite his obvious fear, Logan gambled that Bauer would not pull the trigger, and he was right—Bauer didn't shoot. Logan didn't realize that the entire episode was a ruse to permit Bauer to plant a transmitter on Logan, and that plan worked perfectly.

FINAL MOMENTS

Charles Logan, in an ambulance on a respirator, weakly calls the name of his former wife, Martha Logan. He was seriously injured when he was stabbed by Martha with a kitchen knife when Logan went to see her earlier on Day 6. His mere presence in her home, given their history together, was enough to make Martha lose control and attack Logan without provocation. Her blow sliced an artery, and Logan had to be rushed to hospital.

MARTHA LOGAN

Former First Lady Martha Logan went from being Charles Logan's life partner to the cause of his downfall and death. She was, for a time, his closest adviser, but she also battled mental illness. On Day 5, her life forever changed with the murder of her friend, David Palmer, and she became convinced subsequent events were connected to the assassination. Her husband rejected her concerns, and their relationship splintered when she realized Logan was corrupt, even willing to let her die in a terrorist attack. She and former Secret Service Agent Aaron Pierce therefore helped Jack Bauer bring down Logan's presidency. After Day 5, she divorced Logan and moved into a private mental health facility. On Day 6, however, Logan returned, claiming to be a reformed man assisting a CTU operation. His presence, however, so deeply upset Martha that she went into a rage and stabbed him. She remains confined to her home, while authorities sort out her legal disposition.

BAD NEWS

Martha Logan, having angrily dunked her hair in the sink, is about to encounter bigger problems at 7:28 a.m. on Day 5, as Walt Cummings knocks on her door. He's coming to inform her that David Palmer has been assassinated. The news will send Martha into a struggle to prove that other Day 5 events are connected to Palmer's murder.

PROTECTOR

Martha Logan sits with her partner and protector, former Secret Service Agent Aaron Pierce, while confronting her ex-husband, Charles Logan, at 6:45 p.m. on Day 6. Martha taunted Logan with the fact that she had a close relationship with Pierce, and eventually became so upset by the presence of the former President that, a few minutes later, she got up and impulsively stabbed him with a kitchen knife.

KEY PLAYER

Martha Logan's personal assistant, Evelyn Martin, hands her a copy of a presidential press release covering up the truth behind Walt Cummings death at 2:07 p.m. on Day 5. Evelyn was a key player on Day 5, as she was the inside source of the much sought-after recording that implicated President Charles Logan in wrongdoing.

TAKING ACTION

A terrified Martha Logan, reacts after she instinctively grabs the gun dropped by Agent Adams, one of the Secret Service agents loyal to her husband, and shoots him before he can kill Aaron Pierce in a struggle near the stables at President Logan's retreat. After the shooting, Pierce told Martha to tell no one except Mike Novick what happened, so that Logan would not learn he was still alive.

CLOSE FRIENDS

At 3:54 p.m. on Day 5, Martha Logan and her friend, Anya Suvarov, First Lady of Russia, wait for the Suvarov's motorcade to depart for the airport. Martha knows that Charles Logan has supplied terrorists with the motorcade's route, ostensibly to forestall another nerve gas attack, and that the Suvarovs could be ambushed. She therefore decides to travel with them, hoping her husband will turn the motorcade around before it's too late.

AARON PIERCE

Having joined the United States Secret Service during Ronald Reagan's second term, Aaron Pierce was a senior member of the agency when he retired following Day 5. During that time, he befriended at least one President and one First Lady, and showed great honor and courage. On Day 1, he was assigned to take over the security detail for presidential candidate David Palmer, helped CTU stop two assassination attempts against Palmer, and met Jack Bauer for the first time. On Day 2, he protected now-President Palmer, and when Palmer was removed from office, he helped the President communicate with Bauer, even though doing so got him arrested. Pierce was reinstated after Day 2, and on Day 3 again served as Palmer's bodyguard during another major crisis. On Day 4, he was assigned to protect President Logan, but learned on Day 5 that the President was linked to the Sentox nerve gas conspiracy. He later saved the lives of Martha Logan and the First Couple of Russia, survived an attempt to kill him, and assisted Bauer in proving Logan's guilt.

He then retired, and by Day 6, was romantically involved with Martha Logan.

UNDER ATTACK

Aaron Pierce fires his gun with deadly efficiency at terrorists attempting to invade the limousine carrying Martha Logan, Yuri and Anya Suvarov. Vladimir Bierko's men ambushed the car, disabling it with a shoulder-fired missile, but Pierce managed to have the vehicle turned around enough to prevent a direct hit. He was temporarily knocked out, but woke up just in time. He killed Bierko's men closest to the vehicle, and held the rest off long enough for police to arrive.

FACT FILE

STATUS: Retired

BIRTHPLACE: Classified

MARITAL STATUS:
Widowed;
Romantically linked to Martha Logan

CHILDREN: One son

EXPERIENCE:
Senior Agent, United States Secret Service
(Presidential, Vice Presidential, and special
security details in over 30 years in the Service)

SPECIAL BOND

When Martha Logan divorced Charles Logan after Day 5, Aaron Pierce, newly retired, starting visiting her. Eventually the relationship grew romantic, and he soon became the only one capable of soothing her during periodic rage episodes. Indeed, during Day 6, Pierce calmed her after she attacked Logan, and got her to fulfill her promise to call Russian First Lady Anya Suvarov.

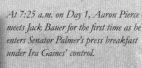

At 7:25 a.m. on Day 1, Aaron Pierce meets Jack Bauer for the first time as he enters Senator Palmer's press breakfast under Ira Gaines' control.

At 5:39 a.m. on Day 2, Aaron Pierce secures a satellite phone for David Palmer, an act for which he was later arrested.

KEY PLAYER

Aaron Pierce's proximity to the nation's leaders has periodically forced him into CTU investigations over the years. On Day 1, when his path crossed with Jack Bauer's for the first time, he was trying to capture or kill Bauer, having been told he was an assassin. On Day 2, Pierce measured his official duty against the greater good when he aided Palmer after he was detained. By Day 5, Pierce was fully dragged into a war for the nation's soul, and he risked his life and career to help make things right.

SECRET SERVICE

The United States Secret Service was established in 1865 as the primary agency responsible for investigating and preventing the counterfeiting of United States Currency. That, and other fraud crimes perpetrated against the Federal Government, remains a primary mission for the agency to this day. But the job of protecting the President, Vice President, their families, former Presidents and Vice Presidents, leading candidates, and their families has grown over the years to be the main focus of the agency. That mission began in 1901, after the assassination of President William McKinley, with the assignment of two full-time bodyguards to the President, and has evolved since to include hundreds of agents.

DISGRACE

A beaten and bound Pierce listens with disgust as Charles Logan tries justifying his illegal actions on Day 5. He told Pierce the evidence implicating him had been destroyed, and that he would let him go only if Pierce would remain silent regarding Logan's misdeeds. Pierce responded by calling Logan a traitor and a disgrace. Logan then wanted him killed, but Pierce managed to escape.

MIKE NOVICK

Mike Novick was a seasoned political operative by the time he became David Palmer's campaign manager, helping Palmer navigate scandal and crisis on Day 1. As President Palmer's Chief of Staff, though, Novick found that counseling the most powerful man in the world is fraught with danger. He made the wrong call on Day 2, for instance, concluding that Palmer's decision to delay retaliating against terrorists was a mistake, and so he assisted the attempt to remove Palmer from office. Novick later realized his error, and helped CTU stop Peter Kingsley, but Palmer still fired him. By Day 4, Novick remade himself as a senior advisor to Vice President Charles Logan. When Logan became president during a terror crisis, Novick convinced him to bring in Palmer to guide the White House response. Then, on Day 5, Novick became Logan's Chief of Staff, and soon learned, to his horror, that the President was also involved in the day's conspiracy. He helped bring down Logan, and left government service after that.

DELICATE SITUATION

Mike Novick gets an update from CTU on the developing crisis at the Ontario Airport early on Day 5, while Walt Cummings and President Charles Logan wait anxiously. When Cummings was later exposed as part of the Day 5 conspiracy, working from inside the administration, Novick took over as Logan's Chief of Staff.

CHIEF OF STAFF

The White House Chief of Staff is the highest-ranking official on the President's executive staff—his most senior aide. The Chief of Staff typically controls access to the President and has strong influence over his daily agenda and staff appointments. There is no Constitutional mandate that a President appoint a Chief of Staff, and indeed, President John F. Kennedy never did. Mike Novick is only the second man in history to serve as Chief of Staff for two presidents. James Baker was the first, having held the job under both Ronald Reagan and George H.W. Bush.

COLLEAGUES

On Day 2, Mike Novick and Lynne Kresge were President David Palmer's top advisers. That changed, however, when Novick decided to support Vice President Prescott's attempt to remove Palmer from office. Novick had Kresge temporarily detained to prevent her from warning Palmer, and she was critically injured trying to escape—a private burden Novick has lived with ever since.

OTHER SENIOR ADVISORS

THOMAS LENNOX

Lennox has an extensive resume as a government policy expert and was an advisor to the David Palmer campaign. But he only came to the White House after Wayne Palmer was elected president, naming Lennox his Chief of Staff. In fact, it was Lennox who talked Wayne into running for president with Noah Daniels on the ticket. On Day 6, he deftly navigated harrowing political waters, battling Palmer over a controversial policy initiative, exposing Reed Pollock's role behind the attempt to kill Palmer, and serving as a buffer between the feuding Palmer and Daniels camps. He initially outflanked Daniels to prevent Palmer's removal from office, but later, after Palmer was incapacitated, served Daniels loyally, and tried to make amends with those he antagonized during the crisis.

Reed Pollack
Pollock was Tom Lennox's Deputy Chief of Staff on Day 6 when he was exposed conspiring to kill President Wayne Palmer. He tried luring Lennox into the plot, assaulted him when he refused, helped smuggle deadly components into the White House bunker, and planted the bomb that injured Palmer. Lennox turned him in, and Pollock tried negotiating a deal to avoid the death penalty.

Walt Cummings
Cummings was President Logan's security chief on Day 4, and initiated the plan to kill Jack Bauer. By Day 5, he was Chief of Staff, but also secretly involved with the Sentox nerve gas conspiracy, convinced the original plan would strengthen American influence abroad. He was exposed, and later found hung to death—a murder passed off as a suicide.

Dr. Arthur Welton
During Day 6, Welton was the senior physician in charge of the White House medical facility who supervised President Wayne Palmer's care. Welton was required to follow the wishes of Palmer's closest family member, Sandra Palmer, when she insisted Palmer be revived from a medically induced coma. As Welton warned, Palmer could not take that much stress, and eventually suffered a cerebral hemorrhage.

Karen Hayes
A former FBI and Homeland Security official who took over CTU on Day 5, Hayes quickly realized that President Charles Logan was the problem, not CTU. After Day 5, she restored the agency, and married Bill Buchanan. By Day 6, she was a special assistant to President Wayne Palmer when massive political fallout hit her, leading to her forced retirement.

Ted Simmons
Simmons was a senior member of President David Palmer's Secret Service security detail on Day 2, when he was asked by Palmer to perform a job outside the scope of his duties—interrogate NSA chief Roger Stanton. Palmer knew Simmons had interrogation experience from his Special Forces background, and asked him to force information from Stanton about the nuclear terror plot.

Lynne Kresge
Kresge, counselor to President David Palmer, was highly suspicious of Deputy NSA Director Eric Rayburn and Sherry Palmer on Day 2. She later broke with Mike Novick over the plan to remove Palmer from office, and tried warning Palmer, but Novick had her illegally detained to prevent that. Kresge tragically fell from a staircase and suffered serious neurological injuries while trying to escape.

Lisa Miller
Miller was Vice President Daniels' senior aide, and lover, on Day 6. She showed great loyalty to Daniels, even offering to perjure herself for him. And yet, she simultaneously carried on another affair, with lobbyist Mark Bishop, a spy for Russian intelligence. Daniels found out and forced her to supply Bishop with false intelligence, but Bishop became suspicious and choked her into unconsciousness.

Elizabeth Nash
Nash was a campaign aide to David Palmer and the daughter of one of his closest friends. On Day 1, she had a tryst with her boyfriend, who was really Alexis Drazen, using her to learn Palmer's itinerary for an assassination attempt. When CTU found out, it had Nash meet with Drazen again under surveillance, but she stabbed Drazen, and he later died from his injury.

Jenny Dodge
Dodge was David Palmer's first presidential press secretary, tasked on Day 2 by Palmer with preventing details about the nuclear terror plot from leaking into the media. It was a job complicated by reporter Ron Wieland, who pursued the story until President Palmer had him detained. Dodge was also at Palmer's side when Mandy tried to kill him as Day 2 concluded.

Dr. Anne Packard
Packard was President David Palmer's full-time physician as he recovered from the assassination attempt at the end of Day 2. She continued caring for him into Day 3, and at some point, also became romantically involved with the President. But a scandal involving Packard's former husband convinced her she could never handle constant media scrutiny, and she ended her relationship with Palmer.

Carl Webb
Webb was a hard-nosed political operative working for Senator David Palmer who once helped Sherry Palmer cover up her son's involvement in a death. On Day 1, it turned out Webb was really working for shadowy financiers who were trying to control Palmer. But Keith Palmer recorded him making incriminating statements, and David Palmer turned the recording over to authorities.

Patty Brooks
Brooks was David Palmer's campaign manager during the Super Tuesday primaries on Day 1, when she became a pawn in Sherry Palmer's struggle with her husband. After being rejected by Palmer, Sherry convinced Patty to make sexual advances toward him, in order to give Sherry leverage, and information about his plans. But Palmer saw through the ruse and fired Brooks on the spot.

JAMES HELLER

James Heller was an influential member of the U.S. defense establishment when President John Keeler appointed him Secretary of Defense. Prior to Day 4, Heller hired Jack Bauer as a special advisor, working closely with Heller's daughter, Audrey Raines, a senior policy analyst whom Bauer eventually fell in love with. All three of them, along with Heller's son, Richard, were pulled into Day 4's events when terrorists abducted Heller and Raines with a plan to broadcast Heller's execution on the Internet. But Bauer intervened, and saved them both. On Day 5, Heller returned to try and force President Charles Logan's resignation. When Christopher Henderson threatened Heller to save himself, Heller drove his car off a cliff to thwart him. Miraculously, Heller survived the crash, and after leaving government to convalesce, he returned briefly to CTU on Day 6 to recover Audrey, and firmly warned Bauer to stay away from his daughter.

SELF SACRIFICE

Late on Day 5, James Heller realizes Henderson's men are targeting him by helicopter. By phone, he instructs Jack Bauer not to let Henderson escape, and decides to sacrifice himself to prevent Henderson from using him as a bargaining chip, driving off a cliff and into a lake. Heller fortunately survived the crash.

HELLERS TARGETED

Audrey Raines was at her father's side when terrorists attacked, kidnapping both of them.

Richard Heller had a difficult relationship with his father, and it became much worse on Day 4.

On Day 4, terrorists strategically used James Heller, his son, Richard, and daughter Audrey Raines, to waste CTU resources while humiliating the United States. Prior to Day 4, the mercenary known as Mandy lured Richard into a sexual encounter with another man that Richard wanted kept private. The purpose of the encounter was to allow Mandy to put a monitoring device into Richard's cell phone to track James Heller's whereabouts, and to place calls to Marwan to confuse investigators. When James Heller and Audrey were kidnapped after visiting Richard, Heller's son came onto CTU's radar as a possible suspect because of suspicious cell phone activity. CTU briefly tortured Richard, and James Heller later permitted the interrogation to resume. Their political differences undoubtedly impacted these developments and Richard's refusal to discuss his tryst with another man was due to the fact that he did not want his father to know about his sexual orientation. He eventually explained things, but the incident further strained their relationship.

After CTU's interrogation techniques failed to get Richard Heller to discuss how terrorists might have gotten into his cell phone, his father confronted him. At that point, Richard finally conceded he must have been duped during a bisexual encounter—information he had tried to conceal.

SECDEF

James Heller was President John Keeler's Secretary of Defense (SecDef is the Secretary's unofficial Armed Forces nickname), and retained the job after Charles Logan replaced Keeler on Day 4 until he was injured in a car crash on Day 5. As SecDef, he was an enormously powerful man—serving in the President's Cabinet as the civilian authority over the United States Armed Forces and supervising the six Joint Chiefs of Staff. Although CTU is a CIA domestic unit, Heller built a close working relationship between CTU and the Department of Defense (DoD). First, he hired Jack Bauer as a special advisor and assigned his daughter, Audrey, to serve as a liaison between the agencies. Then, on Day 4, he temporarily assumed direct oversight of CTU after Erin Driscoll's departure.

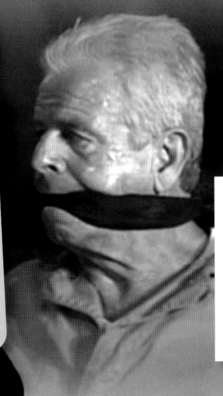

HOSTAGE

As shown across the world on Web-streaming video, terrorists kidnapped James Heller on Day 4 as part of a propaganda ploy to misdirect CTU's attention. They enacted an elaborate plan to put the high-ranking official through a show trial and execution on a global Web broadcast. He and his daughter Audrey continually resisted, however, even attempting a bold escape at one point, and then considering suicide. But Jack Bauer managed to rescue them both.

AUDREY RAINES

Audrey Raines, James Heller's daughter, was a prominent Defense Department analyst when she fell in love with Jack Bauer. On Day 4, Audrey was kidnapped with her father, saved by Bauer, assisted CTU, and then broke off her relationship with Bauer after his actions led to the death of her estranged husband, Paul Raines. Still, when Bauer faked his death and disappeared, she was devastated. On Day 5, working with CTU as a DoD liaison, she learned Bauer was still alive, and helped him get evidence incriminating President Logan to her father. She survived a knifing from Christopher Henderson, and when the crisis passed, she and Bauer hoped to finally be together. But Chinese agents first abducted Bauer, and later Audrey after she went to China to find Bauer. Abused, she was catatonic by the time Cheng Zhi returned her to Bauer as part of an illicit exchange on Day 6. Although she could barely speak, she gave Bauer a crucial clue. But James Heller took Audrey home, and as Day 6 ended Bauer opted to stay away from her to spare her from his dangerous life.

DECEASED

Audrey Raines' Department of Defense (DoD) personnel file was stamped with the word "deceased" before Day 6, after the American government received evidence she was killed in a car accident in China while searching for Jack Bauer. It was all part of an elaborate ruse, however. The Chinese kidnapped Raines, and faked her death to use her as possible future leverage with the American government. They subjected her to ongoing physical and mental abuse before making her a pawn to force Jack Bauer to acquire classified Russian technology.

FACT FILE

STATUS: At home with her father in a semi-catatonic state, traumatized from severe mental and physical abuse.

BIRTHPLACE: Providence, Rhode Island

MARITAL STATUS: Widowed (Paul Raines)

CHILDREN: None

RELATIVES: James Heller (father), Alicia Heller (mother), Susan Heller (step-mother), Richard Heller (step-brother)

EDUCATION:
- Master of Arts, Public Policy, Brown University
- Bachelor of Arts, English, Yale University

EXPERIENCE:
- Department of Defense, Inter-Agency Liaison
- Department of Defense, Senior Policy Analyst
- Anderson Aerospace Corporation, Consultant for Government Contracts
- Ballard Technology, Government Liaison
- Registered Lobbyist
- U.S. House of Representatives, Armed Services Committee, Legislative Assistant

Left: Audrey Raines, deeply wounded, stumbles to Jack Bauer, who saves her life. Below left: Raines later guards Henderson, barely able to restrain herself from shooting him.

DEADLY PLOY

Christopher Henderson uses Jack Bauer's love for Audrey Raines to acquire the Charles Logan audio recording at 12:54 a.m. on Day 5. He sliced Raines' brachial artery, forcing Bauer to give up the recording to save her, which he did by wrapping a makeshift tourniquet around her arm. Raines later found herself with a chance to shoot Henderson, but couldn't bring herself to do it.

DASHED HOPES

At 6:47 a.m. on Day 5, Jack Bauer and Audrey Raines reunite for a quiet moment, optimistic about their future together. Nine minutes later, however, Audrey would discover Bauer missing, abducted by the Chinese, and their happiness likely dashed forever. Both would be imprisoned, psychologically scarred, and separated again at the insistence of her father, James Heller.

HARSH INTERROGATION

At 9:15 p.m. on Day 5, Jack Bauer confronts Audrey Raines about Collette Stenger's accusation that she was Stenger's source inside the Defense Department, and hotel records linking her to Walt Cummings. When Audrey tells Bauer that Stenger is lying, and that her connection to Cummings related to an ill-advised liaison with him, Bauer believes her and backs off.

TRAGIC RELATIONSHIP

At the abandoned Calderone Hotel, Chinese officials hand Audrey Raines over to Jack Bauer, whom she has not seen in almost two years, in return for Bauer delivering the FB sub-circuit board late on Day 6. Bauer removed her gag, looked into her eyes, and apologized to her. He did not yet realize Raines was in a semi-catatonic state and unable to fully process who he was. The reunion was brief, as Raines was instructed to walk away, with Bauer planning to blow the building once she was safe. But CTU intervened—Bauer and Raines were saved, but Chinese official Cheng Zhi escaped with the component.

SENIOR OFFICIALS

Since terrorist plots periodically involve attacks against senior government leadership, it's logical and necessary that CTU routinely interact with the President, the Vice President, Secretary of Defense, various Cabinet members, heads of other intelligence agencies, senior members of Congress, and military leaders. Indeed, since several plots faced by CTU have involved attacks on the President himself, the agency has often found itself pulled into serious power battles within the government. On Day 2, for example, CTU first took orders from President David Palmer, then Vice President James Prescott, and then Palmer again. On Day 4, President John Keeler was replaced by Vice President Charles Logan, and on Day 6, President Wayne Palmer was replaced by Vice President Noah Daniels, then briefly returned to office before lapsing into a coma. CTU has also had growing ties in recent years with the Department of Defense and the Department of Homeland Security.

While the President typically operates out of the White House proper, in a major crisis, he moves into an ultra-secure command bunker underneath the building. On Day 5, Charles Logan worked from the bunker, as did Wayne Palmer on Day 6.

JOHN KEELER

On Day 4, Keeler was David Palmer's Republican opponent during his re-election campaign, fighting an uphill battle against a popular president. Palmer, however, dropped out of the race due to a major scandal, and Keeler captured the White House. On Day 4, as Habib Marwan's terror spree unfolded, Keeler took to the skies on board Air Force One for safety, but a Marwan confederate managed to shoot the plane down. Keeler's son, Kevin, and most of the staff and crew on board the plane were killed, but miraculously, Keeler survived, although he suffered incapacitating injuries. That precipitated his removal from office under the 25th Amendment to the Constitution, and the ascension of Charles Logan to the presidency. Before Keeler, five sitting presidents had survived assassination attempts, but none was as grievously injured as Keeler, and none had to be removed from office, although Ronald Reagan's authority was briefly transferred to Vice President George Bush while he underwent surgery.

KEY PLAYERS

Defense Secretary Ethan Kanin (top photo) and Admiral John Smith (below), Chairman of the Joint Chiefs, both operated from the White House bunker on Day 6. They jointly coordinated the plan to launch a retaliatory nuclear strike in the Middle East strongly favored by Vice President Noah Daniels and by Smith. Then, later, they worked together to manage the precision attack against an oil platform where Phillip Bauer and his Chinese allies took refuge.

ROGER STANTON

Stanton was the National Security Agency (NSA) director on Day 2, and a traitor who helped the Second Wave group smuggle a nuclear device into the country. President David Palmer had Stanton tortured, forcing him to admit the plan was to cause a scare, and then have a secret special-ops team recover the nuke. He claimed he committed the act to force Palmer to toughen his foreign policy.

ERIC RAYBURN

Rayburn was Stanton's Deputy NSA Director on Day 2. He prevented intelligence provided by Jack Bauer about the impending bombing of CTU Los Angeles from reaching CTU and President David Palmer in time to evacuate the facility, reasoning that he couldn't let Bauer's cover with Joseph Wald's organization be compromised during the nuclear crisis. When Palmer found out, he immediately fired Rayburn.

POWER PLAYS

Over the years, high-ranking officials have periodically maneuvered for power in crisis situations. On Day 1, the Secretary of Defense cast the controversial deciding vote to remove David Palmer from office under the 25th Amendment in a situation where the president was not incapacitated, temporarily putting Vice President James Prescott into office. On Day 4, Donald Ashton, Speaker of the House of Representatives, became suspicious of President Logan's move to allow Palmer to advise him on the terror crisis, which potentially interfered with a process that could have put Ashton into the White House. Since President Keeler was incapacitated, Logan, as Vice President, took over, but if it was proven that Logan was incapable of handling the crisis, as Ashton suspected, then he too could have been removed from power. In that scenario, Ashton would have become President, since the Speaker is third in the line of succession.

NOAH DANIELS

As Day 6 began, Vice President Noah Daniels was clearly a hardliner, favoring extreme action in response to the wave of terror attacks wracking the nation. He opposed President Wayne Palmer's decision to delay retaliation, and supported Tom Lennox's initiative to move American Muslims into detention centers. When Palmer was first incapacitated, Daniels planned a nuclear attack in the Middle East, but Palmer awoke in time to counter his actions, and Daniels' next gambit, to have Palmer removed from office, failed. Palmer then ordered him to resign, but before he could do so, Palmer lapsed into a coma, and Daniels again took over. A series of missteps in negotiating with Phillip Bauer during a confrontation with Russia, and in being romantically involved with his aide, who had been compromised by Russian intelligence, seemed to moderate Daniels by the end of Day 6.

JAMES PRESCOTT

Vice President Prescott was the first man to ascend to the presidency twice through the 25th Amendment, "caretake" it, and then return power to the man he replaced, David Palmer. Prescott first briefly took power after spearheading Palmer's removal on Day 2, and later that day, he took over again when Palmer was felled by an assassination attempt. Prescott served after Day 2, until he was himself wounded by terrorists, leading Palmer to return.

CHARLES LOGAN

Vice President Charles Logan was unprepared to handle a terror crisis when John Keeler was incapacitated and removed from office on Day 4, and required help from former President David Palmer. Logan later went on to be only the second man, after Richard Nixon, to resign the presidency after his Day 5 role was exposed. Following David Palmer, on Day 6, he became only the second former president in history to be assassinated.

HAL GARDNER

Gardner was the second man in history to attain the vice presidency and then the presidency without being elected to either office, after Gerald Ford. He became Charles Logan's Vice President after Logan replaced John Keeler. On Day 5, Gardner tried to help Logan manage the nerve gas crisis, strongly urging him to institute martial law. When Logan was forced to resign on Day 5, Gardner served out the rest of Logan's term.

PRESIDENTIAL LOCATIONS

No one knows when, or where, a terror attack might happen, so it's crucial that the President of the United States can command the nation's response from any location. During a nuclear threat on Day 2 President David Palmer moved to a bunker at the Northwest Regional Operations Complex in Oregon. On Day 4, Vice President Charles Logan operated from the White House command bunker, and on Day 6, President Wayne Palmer and Vice President Noah Daniels both ran operations from that same bunker complex. On Day 5, Logan remained at his presidential retreat in Hidden Valley, California, partly to isolate himself as his role in a criminal conspiracy unraveled.

PRESIDENTIAL RETREAT

On Day 5, President Charles Logan worked from his presidential retreat in Hidden Valley, California, which was sometimes called the Western White House. After his disgrace, Logan was later confined there under house arrest. It made a comfortable prison. Built on hundreds of acres of prime real estate, the luxury ranch includes stables, a spacious courtyard with a flowing, 5,000-gallon pond, and a main house featuring a private office and conference room that includes a gigantic, custom-built, redwood conference table.

Office/Study

Conference Room

Hallway

Lounge

Bedroom

Bathroom

WHITE HOUSE BUNKER

When a nuclear crisis dawned on Day 6, President Wayne Palmer relocated operations to the ultra-secure White House command bunker. He took key officials with him including Vice President Noah Daniels, Secretary of Defense Ethan Kanin, advisors Tom Lennox and Karen Hayes, and Admiral John Smith—Chairman of the Joint Chiefs. The bunker includes, among other things, a Presidential command office, high-tech conference room/communications center, private offices, and a sophisticated medical facility.

Corridor

Reed Pollock Office

Karen Hayes and Tom Lennox Office

Corridor

Conference Room

Office of the President

Lounge

Corridor

Blast Doors

Elevator

OVAL OFFICE

Wayne Palmer's Oval Office at the White House was where he began, and ended, his command of the USA on Day 6. Many of his personal effects paid tribute to his late brother—former president, David Palmer. These included a photo of the two brothers together who had secured a place in history as the first siblings to capture the presidency. David Palmer's Medal of Valor was also on display among Wayne's personal effects.

V.I.P. TRANSPORTATION

Unfortunately, U.S. leaders are often potential targets for terrorists, so it isn't surprising that CTU is frequently required to protect and collaborate closely with them as they travel. With the President, Vice President, Cabinet officials, and various candidates for higher office routinely on the go, CTU often has to coordinate or liaise with those arranging their transportation. Thus, Air Force One, Air Force Two, presidential limousines, and helicopters often show up on CTU's mission roster. Indeed, during a crisis, some presidents have found it necessary to command the nation from the skies on board Air Force One, which is fully equipped to support the President and his staff without refueling for up to 7,800 miles at a time. One of CTU's biggest failures, however, was not saving Air Force One on Day 4, when terrorists managed to shoot the plane down.

At 9:09 a.m. on Day 1, a police escort leads the limo carrying Senator David Palmer and his wife, Sherry Palmer, to a campaign appearance. Inside, the Palmers argue over whether to come forward, while voters are still heading to the polls, with information about their son's apparent involvement in a man's death.

HEADING TO AN AMBUSH

A limousine carrying Russian President Suvarov, his wife Anya, and First Lady Martha Logan heads for the airport at 3:58 p.m. on Day 5. Martha Logan knew the vehicle was heading into an ambush, because her husband, President Logan, gave terrorist Vladimir Bierko the motorcade's route to forestall a major nerve gas attack. Hoping Logan would warn the motorcade, she got into the limo with Secret Service Agent Aaron Pierce. Fortunately, Pierce ordered the limo turned around just before a missile struck it. That, combined with the car's armor construction, prevented a direct hit and saved the occupants.

On Day 5, a Navy SH-60B Seahawk filled the role as Marine One. The Seahawk is basically the Navy's version of the Sikorsky H-60 BlackHawk.

Logan waits pensively as Bauer commandeers Marine One. Bauer posed as the co-pilot, stunned Logan's bodyguards, and forced the pilot to land at a designated location.

HIJACKING MARINE ONE

At 6:07 a.m. on Day 5, Jack Bauer sneaks aboard Marine One—in this case, a Navy SH-60B Seahawk helicopter—to commandeer the chopper and interrogate President Logan. Bauer forced the pilot to land near an empty warehouse, where he tried to force a confession from Logan about his relationship to the nerve gas plot. But Bauer had only limited time with Logan, and he knew it, since Marine One—the designation for any aerial vehicle carrying the President outside of Air Force One—had a built-in tracking beacon. It later became clear that Bauer's real gambit was not to gain a confession, but rather, to plant a transmitter on Logan so that CTU could record self-incriminating statements later.

AIR FORCE ONE

President John Keeler, his son, Kevin, staff, and mobile command center soar above the California Desert on board Air Force One shortly before 11 p.m. on Day 4, planning to land momentarily after spending most of the day airborne during Habib Marwan's terror spree. The plane, carrying almost 80 passengers and over 20 crew, was tragically shot down moments later by the stolen Stealth fighter jet commanded by terrorist Mitch Anderson. The event was a cruel strike upon a national icon. The moniker Air Force One actually refers to either of two Boeing 747-200B series aircraft maintained by the Defense Department that are always on standby, and designated as Air Force One, whenever the president is flying.

AIRBORNE COMMAND

Air Force One is designed to include a fully functional command-and-control center for the President of the United States and his associates to operate from for dozens of hours at a time while airborne during a crisis. Here, President Keeler is shown working in his executive office on board the aircraft on Day 4, communicating with CTU and monitoring events on the ground. He stayed airborne on Air Force One much of the day to avoid possible attempts against him while Habib Marwan was on the loose, but that had the effect of giving Marwan's associate, Mitch Anderson, time to implement a plan to steal a Stealth fighter jet and use it to shoot down the plane.

AIR TRAVEL

Franklin D. Roosevelt was the first sitting president to fly in an airplane—a Boeing 314 "flying boat" in 1943. The C-87A Liberator Express, a reconfigured B-24 bomber, was the first airplane officially designated for presidential travel, but in 1944, authorities switched to a C-54 Skymaster, dubbed "The Sacred Cow," for Roosevelt. Harry S. Truman replaced that plane with a C-118 Liftmaster, dubbed Independence, and all subsequent presidents had their own dedicated aircraft after that. John F. Kennedy was the first to use a jet—a Boeing 707 called Special Air Mission (SAM) 2600, which was later called Air Force One—it's official air traffic control designation. The transition to larger 747's occurred during George W. Bush's presidency.

Vice President Noah Daniels ponders his policy dispute with President Wayne Palmer over retaliating for terrorist attacks while returning to Washington D.C. on Air Force Two midway through Day 6.

AIR FORCE TWO

Early on Day 6, Vice President Noah Daniels was traveling on board Air Force Two, returning to Washington D.C., when he learned of the attempt to kill President Wayne Palmer, and that he was now Acting President. Air Force Two, like Air Force One, is simply a term for the official air traffic control designation for any airplane carrying the Vice President. Typically in recent years, Air Force Two has usually been a modified Boeing 757, but periodically, the Vice President is ferried in one of the larger 747's normally reserved for the President, and when that happens, the plane's designation becomes Air Force Two. That was the case on Day 6, when Daniels traveled on board a 747 version of Air Force Two.

DAY 1

Victor Drazen calmly awaits the final encounter with his hated enemy, Jack Bauer. Drazen, a Serbian nationalist and war criminal, and his sons Andre and Alexis, spent years planning revenge on Bauer following the Operation Nightfall military mission in Kosovo two years before Day 1. Indeed, all the day's events centered around Drazen's vendetta to square accounts with Bauer and David Palmer, who had approved Operation Nightfall. The intensely personal nature of the mission would change Jack Bauer's life forever.

KIDNAPPED

The worst day of Jack Bauer's life begins with rare normalcy—a quiet night at home with his family. Within 24 hours, that normalcy would be forever shattered. Bauer's daughter, Kim, sneaks out to meet a friend and two young men who abduct them. Those men are operating on orders from Ira Gaines, a mercenary with orders to assassinate Senator/presidential candidate David Palmer during the California Primary. Just as he hears of Kim's disappearance, Bauer is summoned to CTU to investigate the threat against Palmer, and eventually learns there may be a traitorous mole operating inside the agency. While his wife, Teri, frantically searches for Kim, Bauer is torn between his job and his family. Gaines plots to kill Palmer the next morning, while also abducting Teri Bauer. His plan—to use Teri and Kim as bargaining chips to make Bauer help him kill Palmer.

Kim Bauer and her friend Janet York hide from the men who have abducted them as part of the Drazen conspiracy to get revenge on Jack Bauer and Senator Palmer.

12:43AM	12:57AM	01:53AM	02:39AM

The assassin Mandy flirts with photographer Martin Belkin on board a flight bound for LA. Belkin is due to take pictures of Senator Palmer, and Mandy plans to steal his ID, blow up the airplane, and parachute to safety.	*Kim Bauer and Janet York suddenly realize the two guys they snuck out with, named Dan and Rick, have no intention of bringing them home, although their motives are not yet clear.*	*Just shot in an ambush, a dying CTU Administrative Director Richard Walsh hands Jack Bauer a CTU keycard he has discovered that might lead him to the identity of a mole inside the agency.*	*Senator David Palmer has a clandestine meeting with political operative Carl Webb to discuss how to handle media exposure of sensitve information about his son that could destroy his presidential ambitions.*

02:32am

03:59am

After shooting a police officer, Gaine's hired thug Greg Penticoff tells Bauer to help him escape if he wants to see his daughter alive—hinting at a link between the threat against Senator Palmer and Kim's abduction.

04:02am

After being hit by a car as she fled from her captors, Janet York slips into a coma. She would later awaken, only to be killed by the man posing as her father in order to get closer to the Bauers—Kevin Carroll.

05:05am

Ira Gaines shows up, kills Dan, and forces Rick and Kim Bauer to bury him. As they do so, Kim urges Rick to escape with her—now that it's clear Gaines is a threat to both of them.

05:57am

Teri Bauer receives a call from Nina Myers informing her that the dead body located by CTU was that of the real Alan York, meaning that she is with a dangerous imposter—Kevin Carroll.

HEAVY BURDEN

Senator David Palmer, hoping to score a historic triumph in the Super Tuesday primaries, instead finds himself burdened by knowledge that his wife has conspired to cover up his son's involvement in the death of a man who raped his daughter seven years earlier. While Palmer agonizes over the right course of action and its consequences on both his candidacy and his family, he narrowly escapes the plot against his life. When Jack Bauer saves him from an assassin sent by Ira Gaines, it is the first of two attempts on his life on Day 1. While CTU discovers at least one traitor in its midst, Bauer races to find Gaines and rescue Teri and Kim. As Bauer hunts Gaines, the sons of Serbian war criminal Victor Drazen emerge as the masterminds behind the day's events.

As Super Tuesday dawns, David Palmer ponders the news of a cover-up regarding his son's possible involvement in a death seven years earlier. After talking to his campaign manager, Mike Novick, Palmer decides to make the information public.

06:05AM

Senator David Palmer asks his son, Keith, to join him at a press breakfast where he intends to reveal the truth about Keith's involvement in a scandal. Accusing Palmer of putting his career ahead of his family, Keith declines.

06:19AM

Ira Gaines manipulates Bauer by threatening to kill his wife and daughter. Through an earpiece, Gaines instructs Jack Bauer to steal the CTU keycard reportedly encoded with the name of the assassin targeting Palmer.

07:11AM

Teri Bauer is reunited with her daughter Kim, but both are now prisoners of Ira Gaines, and pawns in his plan to force Jack Bauer to assist him in the assassination of Senator David Palmer.

07:52AM

Believing Bauer to be responsible for an attempt to kill Palmer, agents pin him to the ground. The melee caused Bauer to lose the transmitter connecting him to Gaines, and he feared Gaines would kill his wife and daughter.

05:40AM

IRREVOCABLE SPLIT

Day 1 began full of promise for Sherry Palmer as her ambition to become First Lady of the United States came ever closer to fulfillment. But by the end of the day, David Palmer had a very different message for his stunned wife. Following a sequence of events in which Sherry defied Palmer, manipulated and threatened people, risked lives, and even tried to get her husband to sleep with another woman, Palmer told her he wanted to end their marriage, irrespective of the political consequences. Sherry promised Palmer that she would be back in his life sooner or later. Subsequent events on Days 2 and 3 proved her threats to be well-founded.

08:51AM

Analyst, Jamey Farrell is interrogated after CTU discovers she was working for Gaines, for financial reasons. She refuses to talk until a lawyer arrives, but before that happens, she commits suicide—or so it seems at that time.

09:32AM

Unhappy that Palmer is still alive, Andre Drazen calls Gaines. Drazen threatens to withhold Gaines' payment if action is not taken soon—making it clear that Drazen is running the plot to murder Palmer.

11:08AM

Nina Myers uploads satellite imagery of Ira Gaines' compound to Jack Bauer's PDA as Bauer, using Kevin Carroll as a cover, makes plans to infiltrate the compound and rescue his wife and daughter.

11:54AM

Through a hail of gunfire, Jack attempts to drive away from the terrorist compound with his wife, daughter, and also Rick, who aided their escape. The van was eventually stopped, and they had to fight their way out.

THE DRAZENS

Jack Bauer rescues his family, squares accounts with Ira Gaines, and learns that Gaines' employers, the Drazens, are pursuing a vendetta against him. At CTU, he's summoned to his first meeting with David Palmer. Together, they link their mutual participation in the Operation Nightfall military mission to kill Serbian nationalist, Victor Drazen, two years prior to Day 1's events. CTU gets a lead on Drazen's son, Alexis, and clues point Bauer to the inescapable conclusion that Victor Drazen is alive. Simultaneously, Palmer's situation grows dire as he realizes the men financing his campaign intend to control him, and Drazen's thugs locate Teri and Kim. Their escape leads to a car wreck, and they end up separated. While Kim is safely rescued, Teri, stalked by assassins, is stricken with amnesia.

Jack Bauer seeks an opening to get a lock on Gaines. Bauer won a deadly game of cat-and-mouse with Gaines—killing him, but only after learning that Gaines' employers, the Drazens were his real problem.

01:33pm	01:55pm	02:10pm	02:18pm

Alexis Drazen blows up a house filled with Kevin Carroll's men, and then executes Carroll to keep him silent about the Drazen family. Alexis then took over the plan to kill Senator Palmer.

Dr. Rose Kent learns Teri Bauer was raped, and informs Teri that she had an ovarian cyst burst as a result of the trauma. She also advises her to take a pregnancy test—a test that will later turn out positive.

Jack meets David Palmer for the first time. Palmer believed Bauer wanted him dead for authorizing the failed Operation Nightfall mission, but Bauer explained that Gaines had tried to force him to assassinate the senator.

Covert operative Robert Ellis speaks with Palmer and Bauer about Operation Nightfall. Ellis, the only person who knew they were both connected to the mission, tried to help them, but was murdered by the Drazens.

12:36PM

THE SERBIAN CONNECTION

Victor Drazen was a Serbian nationalist and war criminal who commanded the feared Black Dogs unit of Slobodan Milosevic's Secret Police. Two years before Day 1, Senator David Palmer organized Operation Nightfall, commanded by Bauer, to assassinate Drazen. The mission appeared to succeed, although only Bauer survived. But Drazen was actually taken to a top-secret American military prison. When they learned Victor was alive, Drazen's sons, Andre and Alexis, hatched the Day 1 conspiracy to free their father and take revenge on Bauer and Palmer for the death of their mother and sister.

PRIME SUSPECTS

Andre Drazen

After his mother and sister were killed in Operation Nightfall, and his father imprisoned, Victor Drazen's oldest son conspired to rescue Victor and punish the Americans. The result was the Day 1 plot, which failed when Jack Bauer took bloody revenge on Andre and his father.

Alexis Drazen

Victor Drazen's younger son initiated the backup operation to kill David Palmer after Ira Gaines failed. He murdered Kevin Carroll and used Palmer campaign aide Elizabeth Nash to track Palmer. CTU found him, but Nash stabbed him, and Alexis later died from his wounds.

03:52PM

Carl Webb threatens to frame Keith Palmer for the death of his therapist, George Ferragamo, if he reveals his part in the death of his sister's rapist. But Keith taped their conversation, and gives the tape to his father.

03:55PM

After the car wreck which separates her from her daughter, Teri Bauer develops amnesia. Going into a familiar restaurant, the owner recognizes her and reunites her with her close friend, Dr. Phil Parslow.

04:39PM

When Palmer campaign aide Elizabeth Nash realizes that her boyfriend is in fact Alexis Drazen, she tries to plant a transmitter on him for CTU. Nash eventually wrecked the operation by stabbing Alexis, who later died.

05:59PM

Drazen accomplice Jovan Myovic silently watches Teri Bauer and Dr. Phil Parslow arrive at her house, with plans to kill them both. Teri would be saved about an hour later by the timely arrival of Tony Almeida.

ULTIMATE BETRAYAL

Clues lead Jack Bauer to an ultra-secret military prison and an encounter with prisoner Victor Drazen. Drazen's sons soon free him and capture Bauer, and separately, his daughter, although Tony Almeida saves Teri Bauer. The Drazens use Kim to force Bauer to help them hit David Palmer after he wins the day's elections, but Bauer saves Palmer once again. Nina Myers, meanwhile, reveals herself as a traitor and warns the Drazens that Palmer survived. Kim escapes, but word doesn't reach Jack in time. Convinced his daughter was murdered, and driven by rage, he assaults the Drazen's location, kills them all, and races to CTU to stop Nina. However, before he arrives, Nina kills Teri Bauer who has also uncovered Nina's duplicity. The worst day of Jack's life culminates in grief and despair as he cradles his pregnant wife's lifeless body—his life destroyed.

When Teri Bauer encounters Nina Myers in CTU's transformer room, she overhears Myers speaking to her handler and planning her escape, and notices a suspicious pool of blood. Myers pretends to assuage her concerns, but moments later she ties Teri up and shoots her.

07:54PM

Jack Bauer and DoD prison warden Mark DeSalvo question Victor Drazen about the day's events, and Bauer implores Drazen to call off the vendetta against his family.

08:19PM

After being rescued by his sons, Victor Drazen turns the tables on Jack and holds him prisoner. He plans to use Jack to force CTU to back off and allow him to make his escape.

08:59PM

When a vehicle driven by terrorists smashes into Kim Bauer's police escort, she is taken prisoner once again—this time by Drazen's henchmen. She later manages to escape and is reunited with her father.

10:29PM

Forced to bring Senator Palmer a phone for a private call with Victor Drazen, Jack Bauer senses a double-cross. He throws the phone out the window—thwarting an assassination attempt as it immediately explodes.

11:31PM

10:59PM

Nina Myers, using the name Yelena and speaking Serbian, calls Andre Drazen to inform him that Palmer survived the assassination attempt—revealing that she is the deep-cover mole inside CTU.

11:20PM

Although Victor Drazen attempts to surrender, a vengeful Jack Bauer, believing that his daughter is dead, fires multiple rounds into him, thereby ending their blood feud once and for all.

11:53PM

After realizing she had betrayed him, Jack Bauer catches up with Nina Myers as she attempts her escape from CTU. He struggles to prevent himself from killing her on the spot.

11:58PM

As Day 1 draws to a close, Jack Bauer is reunited with his daughter at CTU, after thinking she was dead. His relief was short-lived—a minute later he would discover his wife murdered at the hands of Nina Myers.

DAY 2

18 months later ...

President David Palmer sits uneasily as the leader of the free world 18 months after Day 1. CTU learns a Middle Eastern terror cell is plotting to detonate a nuclear bomb in Los Angeles, and races to prevent disaster. The seriousness of the threat forces Jack Bauer to work with the woman who destroyed his life, Nina Myers, and Palmer to seek help from the woman trying desperately to bring down his presidency—his former wife, Sherry.

NUCLEAR THREAT

After 18 months of inactivity since his wife's murder, a nuclear terror threat against the U.S. from the mysterious Second Wave group brings a reluctant Jack Bauer back to CTU. Early on Day 2, events turn ugly—Bauer murders a suspect under interrogation in order to infiltrate a group affiliated with Second Wave; that group launches a deadly attack on CTU itself; CTU's Special Agent in Charge, George Mason, is fatally poisoned; Kim Bauer's life is threatened by her employer—and that's just the beginning of the madness. Perhaps most devastating of all, Jack learns that the only path to stopping the attack is through his enemy—Nina Myers. Specially released from prison to help, Nina enters into a deadly game of chicken with Jack. While Bauer angles to use Myers to find Second Wave mastermind Syed Ali, Nina hunts for a way to escape custody and kill Jack.

08:36AM	08:49AM	09:00AM	10:16AM

At President David Palmer's request, Jack Bauer returns to CTU early on Day 2, for the first time since his wife's death. Bauer didn't want to be there, but he stayed due to the serious nature of the terror threat.	During an interrogation, Jack shoots and kills suspect Marshall Goren. With time of the essence, Bauer decided to kill Goren in order to make his attempt to infiltrate Joseph Wald's operation seem more realistic.	Megan Matheson is protected from her abusive father, Gary by her nanny, Kim Bauer. Kim didn't know Matheson had already killed the girl's mother. She and Megan escaped, but Matheson tracked them down.	CTU Special Agent in Charge George Mason joins a raid at an industrial complex where Second Wave terrorists assembled the nuclear device, and is exposed to Plutonium residue. He soon realizes his life is in danger.

01:34pm

Agent Miller takes charge of Nina Myers early on Day 2 on orders from George Mason, who was concerned Jack Bauer would kill her. Bauer forced Myers to help him track Syed Ali, but she later made a desperate escape.

Syed Ali

Syed Ali was an Islamic radical who funded and ran the Second Wave operation. Jack Bauer forced him to talk, but he was murdered by Jonathan Wallace to prevent him from exposing the Cyprus recording as a fake.

Gary Matheson

Kim Bauer worked for Gary Matheson, a violent psychopath. He later killed his wife, threatened Kim and his daughter, and murdered a policeman before Kim shot him in self-defense.

PLUTONIUM POISONING

George Mason inhaled Plutonium residue during a raid where the Day 2 nuclear device was assembled. It meant a death sentence as Mason was given 24 hours to live, although normally, the toxic effects would take much longer. Plutonium emits alpha radiation and low-energy X-rays, but the radiation can only be ingested if it's inhaled or absorbed through a wound. That can lead to the onset of cancer over many years.

10:54am

Despite Jack Bauer's efforts, a massive explosion rips through CTU as Joseph Wald's gang manages to attack the facility. It is part of a strategy to interfere with CTU's investigation of Second Wave.

11:54am

George Mason halts the evacuation of the mortally wounded Paula Schaeffer from CTU, and insists that doctors revive her so she can decrypt crucial intelligence related to CTU's pursuit of the nuclear bomb.

12:34pm

Tony Almeida confronts Reza Naiyeer about data linking him and Warner Enterprises to Syed Ali. Naiyeer raised the suspicions of Kate Warner and CTU early on, but the real terrorist contact was his fiancée, Marie Warner.

01:09pm

Jack Bauer interrogates Nina Myers, trying to force her to give him information about Syed Ali. Bauer tries to make her fear he will kill her for revenge if she doesn't cooperate.

HIGH STAKES

Deceit inside Palmer's Administration is revealed when President David Palmer reluctantly allows his former wife, Sherry, back into his inner circle. She produces evidence that NSA Director Roger Stanton activated the Coral Snake special ops unit to help Second Wave threaten the nation. Palmer orders a brutal interrogation of Stanton, who in turn reveals Sherry's role in the conspiracy. Meanwhile, Coral Snake goes after Jack Bauer and Nina Myers, and after their harrowing escape, Nina forces President Palmer to grant her a pardon, in advance of her intended murder of Jack. Myers' information allows Jack to save Kate Warner's life, and get her help in capturing Syed Ali. Bauer brutally manipulates Ali into revealing that the bomb will be launched from Norton Airfield. CTU then learns that Kate's sister, Marie Warner, is connected to Second Wave, and is on the loose.

03:43PM

On a transport plane, in custody, Nina Myers murders her contact to Second Wave, Mamud Rashed Faheen. She did it to give herself bargaining leverage by silencing CTU's only other source on Syed Ali.

04:33PM

Syed Ali torments Kate Warner by making her watch the torture of private investigator Paul Koplin in a cruel attempt to discover what she and Koplin learned from the data on Reza Naiyeer's computer.

04:40PM

Nina Myers' plan was to force President Palmer to sign a pardon and then murder Bauer. She manages to grab a rifle and gets Jack Bauer in her sights, but she is surrounded by CTU snipers.

05:28PM

Kim Bauer and her boyfriend, Miguel, escape from police custody by causing the police car transporting them back to LA to crash. After talking to her father, Kim wants to avoid going back into the nuclear threat zone.

President Palmer confronts Roger Stanton with evidence against him, and offers an immunity deal to reveal what he knows about the nuclear bomb conspiracy. Stanton denied involvement, and Palmer reluctantly ordered Secret Service agent Simmons to torture him.

06:30PM

SHERRY PALMER

Sherry Palmer storms back into her ex-husband's life when she shows up at his bunker offering to use her contacts to investigate a possible plot to undermine Palmer inside his own administration. Of Course, Sherry had an agenda all her own, and presidential advisor Lynne Kresge advised President not to trust her. Palmer had misgivings from the start, but he gave Sherry access after she provided valuable intelligence on Roger Stanton. Only later would he learn that Sherry had initially worked with Stanton and Peter Kingsley to destroy his presidency.

PRESIDENTIAL PARDONS

As distasteful as it was, President David Palmer was well within his legal rights to give Nina Myers a full presidential pardon for her many crimes, in return for her cooperation. That's because all presidents are exclusively granted the power to pardon under Article II, Section 2, of the United States Constitution. The clause gives him sole authority to grant "reprieves and pardons for offenses against the United States, except in cases of impeachment." In modern times, presidents usually only use the power near the end of their term in office, but legally, they can do so at any time, and they cannot be reversed, under any circumstances.

05:32PM

Syed Ali's subordinate, Mohsen, is torturing Kate Warner when Jack Bauer comes to the rescue. Before he can be questioned about Ali's location, Mohsen commits suicide by swallowing a cyanide capsule.

05:58PM

Marie Warner reveals her true self as a committed terrorist when she shoots and kills her fiancée, Reza Naiyeer, after he discovers she was responsible for using his computer to aid Second Wave.

06:59PM

Jack Bauer soon realizes that the body found in a mosque is not that of Syed Ali, and initiates a search of the facility. Bauer captured Ali a short time later in the mosque's basement.

07:32PM

Jack Bauer forces Syed Ali to watch his family apparently being prepared for execution on a video monitor as part of his tactic to break Ali and gain information about the nuclear bomb.

CORAL SNAKE

Jack Bauer rescues Kate Warner in her home from thugs robbing her while she has the microchip evidence in her possession. The microchip was damaged during the fight, forcing Bauer to seek other evidence regarding the Cyprus recording.

Jack captures Marie Warner and the nuclear bomb at Norton Airfield. The device can't be disarmed, so Bauer plans to crash it in an unpopulated area. He bids farewell to his daughter, but George Mason sacrifices himself instead, saving thousands of lives, including Jack's. President Palmer considers attacking the countries implicated by the Cyprus recording, but Syed Ali insists the recording is fake, just before Coral Snake leader, Jonathan Wallace, murders him. Bauer, with help from an Arab agent, confronts Wallace, who offers evidence needed to stop the war, but wants Kate Warner's life in return.

This tattoo indicates the commando was a member of the secret Coral Snake special ops unit who reports directly to the National Security Agency (NSA).

08:06 PM

Loner, Lonnie McRae comforts Kim Bauer after giving her shelter in his cabin in the woods of the Angeles Crest National Forest. McRae tried to force Kim to stay with him, but eventually let her go.

08:22 PM

Agent Goodrich and Bauer find murdered Coral Snake commandos inside a fuel depot at Norton Airfield. They later discover that Jonathan Wallace killed his own men to ensure they wouldn't stop the nuclear bomb launch.

09:42 PM

Jack Bauer interrogates Marie Warner about the location of the bomb. She first refused to talk, and then attempted to misdirect Bauer, but he realized the deception and initiated an emergency search of the airfield.

09:59 PM

A Nuclear Emergency Support Team works frantically to disarm the nuclear device, but quickly ascertains the trigger is tamper proof, causing Jack Bauer to form a desperate plan to move the bomb to an unpopulated area.

03:55AM

PRIME SUSPECTS

Marie Warner

Kate Warner's younger sister was an unlikely member of Syed Ali's sleeper cell, proving willing to betray or murder anyone to help him. She met Ali while living in Europe, and secretly joined his group. Jack apprehended Marie, and she's now in Federal custody.

Ronnie Stark

Stark worked for Peter Kingsley, hunting evidence linking Kingsley to Second Wave. He went after Jack, seeking the incriminating microchip, and tortured Bauer to the brink of death. He failed to get results, and was killed and replaced by Raymond O'Hara.

NEST

Nuclear Emergency Support Teams (NEST) were first established by the Federal Government in the 1970s to provide technical assistance to law enforcement and emergency response teams in the event they became involved in a nuclear incident. Currently run by the Department of Energy, NEST consists of thousands of Federal employees with expertise related to the safe handling of nuclear equipment or material. Since the September 11 attacks, NEST has had a raised profile, and the teams are routinely utilized to patrol major urban areas, taking readings and following up on reports about radioactive or nuclear materials.

10:07PM

Chief of Staff, Mike Novick outlines options for detonating the bomb in a safe area to President Palmer and his advisers. He explains that it will be a suicide mission for the pilot.

10:43PM

George Mason, dying from radiation poisoning, hides in the cockpit of the Cessna and insists on taking Bauer's place on the suicide mission. Bauer stayed with Mason until just before impact, and then parachuted to safety.

12:19AM

Jack meets with Jonathan Wallace, who admits working to help Second Wave. Wallace promises to give proof of his employer's culpability if Jack will hand over Kate Warner, but he is shot before he can reveal too much.

01:55AM

Jack Bauer retrieves a microchip from inside Jonathan Wallace's dead body. The chip contained data about the plot to falsify the Cyprus recording, and Bauer had to get it to CTU immediately to prevent a major war.

CONSPIRACY UNRAVELED

07:38AM

As Day 2 ends, Kim Bauer has a final confrontation with Gary Matheson, Jack races to prevent war, and President Palmer is removed from office after hesitating to retaliate. Bauer, Kate Warner, and Arab agent Yusuf Auda try to get evidence discrediting the Cyprus recording to CTU, but Kate and Yusuf are caught in a riot—Yusuf is killed and thugs damage the evidence and threaten Kate. Meanwhile, Bauer is captured and tortured on orders from Peter Kingsley, the businessman trying to help Second Wave. Bauer escapes, rescues Kate, locates the audio expert behind the recording, and then finds Sherry Palmer trying to hide her connection to Kingsley. He then uses Sherry to find Kingsley, who is killed in a shootout. War is averted, but another attempt is made to assassinate President Palmer.

02:26AM

Kingsley's henchman, Ronnie Stark, brutally tortures Jack Bauer in an effort to force him to hand over the incriminating microchip. But Bauer wouldn't talk, and almost died before finally managing to escape.

03:59AM

Vice President Prescott convenes the Cabinet, without inviting President Palmer, to discuss whether Palmer is unfit to continue in office and whether the 25th Amendment should be invoked.

04:54AM

Secret Service Agent Aaron Pierce escorts President Palmer out of the Cabinet meeting, moments after being removed from office by a one-vote margin under the provisions of the 25th Amendment.

04:59AM

Sherry Palmer shows up at audio technician Alex Hewitt's loft, and runs into Jack Bauer, who is also searching for Hewitt. Bauer would force Sherry to help him find and expose Peter Kingsley.

AMBUSH

At 7:37 a.m. Jack Bauer was able to take out most of Peter Kingsley's bodyguards in a single ambush from his sniper position. The strategy risked Sherry Palmer's life, but left the severely weakened Bauer just one of Kingsley's men and Kingsley himself to deal with.

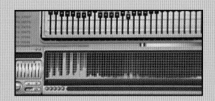

CLEVER FAKE

The Cyprus recording fabricated by audio engineer Alex Hewitt had to be extremely sophisticated in order to pass government audio authentication tests, and it almost led the United States into war. Government tests normally use a variety of computer tools to analyze starts, stops, speed fluctuations, variations in dialogue, background noise, environmental changes, and foreground noise to ascertain if source recordings have been fraudulently spliced together. However, in this case CTU and other experts were unable to detect such anomalies—thanks to Hewitt's use of state-of-the-art proprietary software tools and a delicate touch.

Near the end of Day 2, Jack uses a sniper rifle to fire on Peter Kingsley's men from a tower at the L.A Coliseum. While Kingsley met below with Sherry Palmer, Bauer uses the element of surprise to kill all but one of Kingsley's men.

PETER KINGSLEY

Kingsley helped a mysterious business consortium use the Second Wave plot to try and ignite a Middle Eastern war and drive up oil prices. When CTU disrupted that plan, he tried to shut down his operation, but Jack lured him into a final confrontation.

MAX

This German arms dealer was one of Kingsley's behind-the-scenes partners on Day 2. When the conspiracy failed, Max tried to have President Palmer assassinated. He was eventually killed by Jack approximately six months after Day 2.

05:56AM

Late in Day 2, Kim Bauer shoots and kills Gary Matheson while speaking to her father on a cell phone. Jack Bauer calmed his terrified daughter and convinced her she needed to pull the trigger.

06:54AM

During a phone call from Sherry Palmer to Peter Kingsley, Jack utilizes Alex Hewitt's voice reproduction software to make Kingsley think he is speaking to Hewitt and thereby setting up their final confrontation.

07:41AM

After a brutal fight at the Los Angeles Coliseum, Peter Kingsley takes aim at a weakened Bauer. Before Kingsley could squeeze the trigger, a CTU helicopter arrived and fired on Kingsley, killing him instantly.

7:56AM

On orders from the mysterious operative Max, the assassin Mandy clasps David Palmer's hand— transmitting a dangerous biological agent that almost killed Palmer at the end of Day 2.

DAY 3

Three Years Later …

A desperate Nina Myers makes her stand moments before a final, fatal reckoning with Jack Bauer. Nina interfered with Bauer's attempt to secure the deadly Cordilla Virus, tried to kill him, wreaked havoc on CTU's computer network, killed several members of the CTU medical staff, and threatened to kill Kim Bauer before finally meeting justice. Bauer killed her as she reached for her gun or at least, that is how the event was described in the official CTU record of the incident.

UNDERCOVER

On Day 3, CTU confronts a major bioterrorism threat which appears to involve rogue scientists selling a deadly virus to terror networks. To track them, Jack Bauer goes undercover inside the Salazar drug cartel in Mexico—an organization he had previously infiltrated to bring it's leader Ramon Salazar to justice, at the cost of a heroin addiction. Bauer's plan is to prove he's gone rogue by breaking Salazar out of prison, and then use the Salazars to flush out the sellers. But Bauer's partner, Chase Edmunds—the man Kim Bauer has secretly fallen in love with—pursues Bauer to prevent his "betrayal". Meanwhile, Ramon's brother, Hector Salazar, misdirects authorities into pursuing a false lead; Bauer's only two allies inside CTU—Tony Almeida and Gael Ortega—suffer for helping him; and Bauer and Salazar barely survive a bloody prison riot and military pursuit before escaping into Mexico.

05:35PM

01:08PM	**01:52PM**	**02:07PM**	**3:58PM**

A decomposed body contaminated with a genetically engineered strain of a deadly pneumatic virus is dumped at the National Health Services building in LA, apparently as a threat from an unknown source.	*Jack Bauer prepares a shot of heroin, to satisfy the habit he picked up undercover. A call from his daughter stopped Bauer from shooting up, but he battled the addiction throughout Day 3.*	*Kim finally confesses to her father that she is involved in a relationship with her partner, Chase Edmunds. She knew Jack would worry that Chase's job would put her in even more danger than she had already experienced.*	*Jack tends to Tony Almeida seconds after he was shot in the neck by Salazar henchman David Gomez. Tony was attempting to take Salazar's pawn, Kyle Singer, into custody at the Los Feliz Mall.*

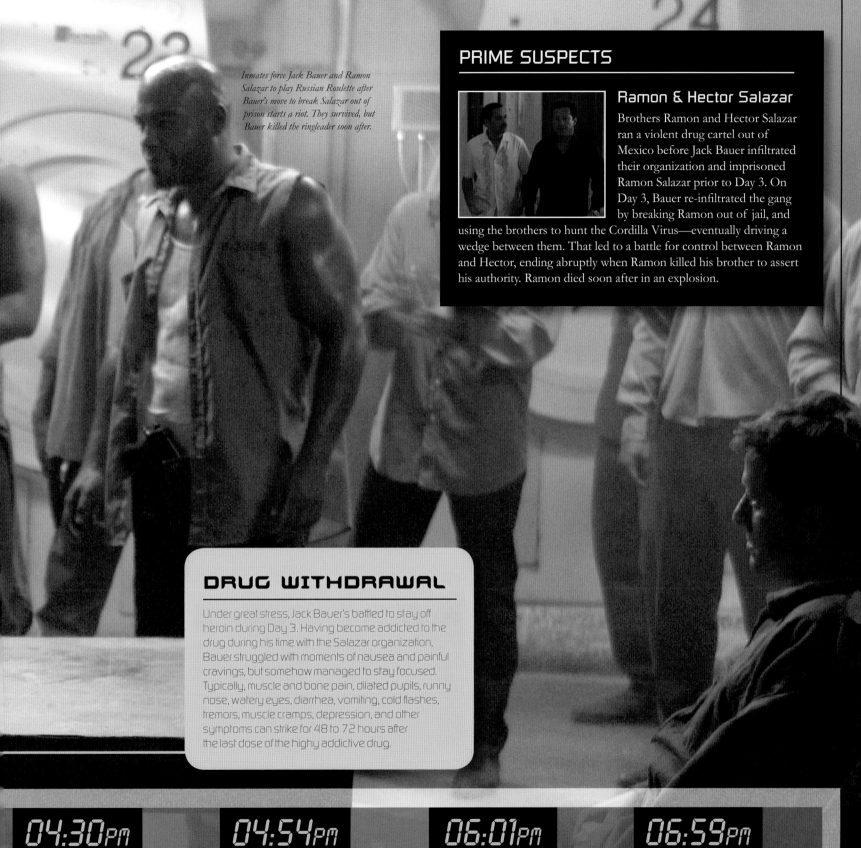

Inmates force Jack Bauer and Ramon Salazar to play Russian Roulette after Bauer's move to break Salazar out of prison starts a riot. They survived, but Bauer killed the ringleader soon after.

DRUG WITHDRAWAL

Under great stress, Jack Bauer's battled to stay off heroin during Day 3. Having become addicted to the drug during his time with the Salazar organization, Bauer struggled with moments of nausea and painful cravings, but somehow managed to stay focused. Typically, muscle and bone pain, dilated pupils, runny nose, watery eyes, diarrhea, vomiting, cold flashes, tremors, muscle cramps, depression, and other symptoms can strike for 48 to 72 hours after the last dose of the highly addictive drug.

04:30 PM

Kyle Singer was captured by Salazar thugs and placed inside a chamber, possibly infected with the virus. When Singer was rescued he learned that he was not infected—the incident was manufactured to distract CTU.

04:54 PM

Jack Bauer attempts to talk his way past Warden Mitchell and walk Ramon Salazar out of prison. Mitchell let them pass, but a short time later, a riot broke out, upsetting Bauer's plan.

06:01 PM

CTU District Director Ryan Chappelle takes command of CTU after Tony Almeida's shooting. Chappelle immediately asked military authorities to intercept and shoot down the helicopter carrying Jack and Salazar.

06:59 PM

Agent Gael Ortega draws his weapon on Kim Bauer after she discovers him monitoring her father's abduction. It later transpired that he was actually working with Bauer to help him infiltrate the Salazar organization.

SCANDAL

Developments spiral out of control both in the field and at the highest levels of power. In Mexico, Jack Bauer grapples for control of the virus with the Salazars, weapons dealer Michael Amador, and his nemesis, Nina Myers. Chase Edmunds joins the fray, complicating events in a way that will eventually leave both Salazar brothers dead, Myers in custody, and the virus still unaccounted for. Simultaneously, President David Palmer battles scandals that threaten to end his re-election bid, including one involving his brother, Wayne, and the return of Sherry Palmer. When Sherry becomes embroiled in the death of a campaign contributor, the Palmer Administration teeters, while CTU desperately races to halt release of the virus.

Knowing that Alan Milliken could destroy David Palmer, Sherry withholds his medication and holds back his wife Julia, when Milliken goes into heart failure. Although she had wanted to gain favor with her estranged husband, ultimately this initiated a chain reaction that would destroy David Palmer's presidency and end the lives of both Julia and Sherry.

01:46AM

08:16PM

Bauer, struggling with heroin withdrawal symptoms, faces Hector Salazar's wife, Claudia, with whom he had an affair when he was undercover. She accused him of betraying her, but Jack helped her attempt to escape.

08:51PM

Dr. Anne Packard informs David Palmer that she will end their relationship after witnessing the suicide of her former husband, Ted Packard. She told Palmer that she could no longer handle the pressure of big-time politics.

08:55PM

After pursuing Bauer to Mexico, Chase Edmunds is captured by the Salazars while believing that Bauer has betrayed CTU. Bauer had to brutally prove his loyalty, at Chase's expense, to maintain his cover.

09:22PM

Jack Bauer leads the Salazars to an auction to purchase the virus from Michael Amador's organization, only to discover that his competition for the deadly product will come from Nina Myers.

LAST STRAW

Ted Packard threatens suicide in front of his former wife, Anne Packard at 8:22 p.m. Ted had implicated Anne in financial improprieties, but he later produced evidence clearing her name before killing himself—an event that drove Anne to end her romantic relationship with President David Palmer.

09:30PM

President Palmer is told by contributor Alan Milliken that his brother and Chief-of-Staff, Wayne Palmer, had an affair with Milliken's wife, Julia. He demands that Wayne be fired or there will be serious consequences.

11:17PM

Sherry Palmer returns to President Palmer's life to handle a dirty job—to get information about Alan Milliken to use as leverage to prevent Milliken from derailing Palmer's health care bill and the career of his brother, Wayne.

11:57PM

Hector Salazar lies dying after being shot by his older brother Ramon for opposing Ramon's risky decision to follow through with stealing the virus from Michael Amador.

12:54PM

Jack and Chase Edmunds confront Ramon Salazar holding a cylinder filled with the virus. Unaware that Amador has booby-trapped it, Bauer demands that Salazar puts the cylinder down. It explodes, killing him.

VIRUS UNLEASHED

Horror strikes as Day 3 marches forward. CTU eventually uncovers Stephen Saunders as the mastermind behind the virus plot, However, Saunders proves perfectly willing to use his biological weapon—unleashing it at the Chandler Plaza Hotel, leading to the death of Gael Ortega and almost 1,000 other people. CTU, in its desperation to find Saunders, is again outsmarted by the renegade Nina Myers when she compromises the agency's computer system and tries a bloody escape attempt. Jack Bauer eventually deals harsh justice to Myers, and appears to close in on Saunders, but not before CTU official Ryan Chappelle is forced to make the ultimate sacrifice.

In accordance with Saunders instructions, Jack Bauer takes Ryan Chappelle to a deserted train yard.

06:56AM

01:56AM

Chloe O'Brian manages to defeat the computer worm planted in CTU's network by Nina Myers just in time to prevent CTU's reluctant release of Myers in return for the kill code to stop a full network shutdown.

02:48AM

CTU interrogators insert a needle into Nina Myers to force information from her. The plan went awry when Nina intentionally pushed the needle into an artery. The rush for emergency medical care allowed her to escape.

02:57AM

Kim Bauer faces off with Nina Myers in a CTU tech room after stumbling into Nina trying to make her escape. Seconds later, Jack Bauer would burst in, dismiss his daughter, and finally kill Myers.

03:55AM

A Russian-made detonation unit containing a vial of the deadly Cordilla Virus sits ready to be activated shortly after being placed near the Chandler Plaza Hotel's ventilation system by terrorist Marcus Alvers.

In the gloom of an anonymous train yard, Jack Bauer does the unthinkable—he gives in to the demands of terrorist Stephen Saunders and shoots an innocent man. It is the only way to convince Saunders to delay releasing the Cordilla Virus.

PRIME SUSPECT

Stephen Saunders

Saunders was a former British soldier who survived Jack Bauer's Operation Nightfall mission and became bitter toward the U.S. government. He masterminded the Cordilla Virus plot to force America to change its foreign policy, but Bauer used Saunders' daughter to capture him and unravel the plot. The widow of one of his victims, Gael Ortega, later murdered Saunders at CTU.

HAZMAT

Before the Cordilla Virus was unleashed at the Chandler Plaza Hotel, Michelle Dessler's CTU team entered the facility without waiting for HAZMAT (Hazardous Materials) units to arrive to provide protective suits as they raced to prevent release of the virus. It was released, and almost 1,000 people died. Once a HAZMAT squad arrived under direction from Dr. Nicole Duncan, the hotel was locked down and no one went in from that point forward without wearing a fully encapsulating, airtight protective suit and independent breathing apparatus.

04:20AM	05:39AM	05:45AM	06:30AM

Stephen Saunders takes a call from Michael Amador as Amador flees from Jack Bauer. Saunders, who had a history with Bauer, was revealed for the first time to be the mastermind behind the horrific plot.

Despite the risk of contamination, Michelle Dessler comforts infected CTU colleague Gael Ortega moments before the Cordilla Virus claims his life at the Chandler Plaza Hotel.

An assault helicopter dispatched by Stephen Saunders rains machine gun fire into an office building containing the MI-6 office where Jack Bauer and MI-6 agent Trevor Tomlinson are sifting through clues to Saunders' location.

A man named William Cole, who managed to slip out of the Chandler Plaza Hotel, returns home to discover his nose is bleeding—the first symptom of a Cordilla Virus infection that could lead to a massive outbreak.

EDGE OF DISASTER

Heroic sacrifices decide the outcome on Day 3. CTU first tries to use Stephen Saunders' daughter to capture him, but he instead kidnaps Michelle Dessler and manipulates Tony Almeida into committing treason to save her. Simultaneously, attempts to cover up the Alan Milliken affair result in Sherry Palmer's murder and the halting of President Palmer's re-election bid. Jack Bauer, meanwhile, helps Almeida rescue Dessler, captures Saunders, and forces from him the locations of his couriers. Saunders is murdered at CTU, leaving one courier at large. Bauer and Chase Edmunds track him down, and thanks to a selfless sacrifice by Edmunds, they prevent an unimaginable disaster.

07:53 AM

Jack Bauer confronts Jane Saunders and explains her father's culpability in the terror plot. He asks for her help in getting in touch with Saunders before millions more die.

08:54 AM

Stephen Saunders sends this video image of Michelle Dessler being held hostage and threatened to Tony Almeida. He uses it as leverage to convince Almeida to help him get his daughter released from CTU.

09:32 AM

Sherry Palmer attempts to betray her former husband by offering Senator John Keeler evidence regarding the death of Alan Milliken—evidence he can use to force President Palmer from the presidential race.

10:55 AM

Tony Almeida fires furiously at Stephen Saunders' men while Michelle Dessler and Jane Saunders duck for cover as CTU's raid on Almeida and Saunders' prisoner exchange goes horribly wrong.

PRIME SUSPECTS

Michael Amador
Amador attempted to sell the Cordilla Virus in a private auction on Day 3, after having already sold it to Stephen Saunders. When his greedy plan to earn extra millions led CTU closer to Saunders, Saunders murdered Amador with a car bomb.

Marcus Alvers
Alvers was the link between Stephen Saunders and Michael Amador. He planted the Cordilla Virus at the Chandler Plaza Hotel, and in so doing, became infected. There, he gave Michelle Dessler information on Saunders and she agreed to shoot him before the disease made him suffer.

Arthur Rabens
Rabens was the last of Stephen Saunders' virus couriers. He managed to slip through CTU's net after Saunders was killed, and tried to release the virus inside a school. Fortunately Jack Bauer and Chase Edmunds were able to stop him at the last possible moment.

11:30AM

A barely conscious Chase Edmunds watches Jack Bauer shoot Arthur Rabens dead just before Rabens can fire on Edmunds. Chase, however, had the virus distribution device locked to his arm and had to make a fateful decision in the next few minutes.

10:57AM

Stephen Saunders' escape helicopter is blown to bits by Marine F-18 fighter jets called in by Jack Bauer. The blast knocks Saunders to the ground, giving Bauer time to capture him.

11:57AM

A weeping Wayne Palmer cradles Julia Milliken's dead body in his arms seconds after she killed Sherry Palmer and herself following Wayne's failed attempt to take incriminating evidence from Sherry.

12:39PM

In a skirmish with virus courier Arthur Rabens, Chase Edmunds ends up with the virus container's detonation device locked onto his arm. Edmunds had Jack Bauer chop his hand off to secure the virus before detonation.

12:53PM

A solemn President Palmer speaks to Jack Bauer by phone to thank him for saving countless lives, and informs him he will not be seeking re-election following Day 3's tragic events.

DAY 4

18 months later …

Jack Bauer slips quietly into hiding after faking his death at the end of Day 4 following his work to bring an end to Habib Marwan's reign of terror. Bauer's heroic efforts aside, he caused an international incident at the Chinese Consulate searching for leads, resulting in a Chinese demand for his arrest and imprisonment. Rogue elements in the U.S. government, determined to silence his knowledge of sensitive secrets, plotted his death, forcing Bauer to attempt the desperate ploy.

CHAOS ERUPTS

Jack Bauer's retirement from fieldwork ends with a train bombing and the kidnapping of Bauer's new boss, Secretary of Defense James Heller, and his daughter, Audrey Raines, who is also in a relationship with Jack. The kidnappings, coordinated by a terrorist named Omar, are designed to humiliate the United States, while the train attack was staged to steal the Dobson Override Device—technology that would enable the terrorists to seize control of nuclear power plants. Bauer follows an operative he hopes will lead him to Omar, and secures information that results in a Special Forces rescue mission that saves Heller and Raines and terminates Omar. Meanwhile, CTU works furiously to prevent nuclear disaster, and an unlikely terrorist sleeper cell—a suburban family—assists Omar's superior, Habib Marwan.

WEB HAVOC
Andrew Paige, Chloe O'Brian's former classmate and an accomplished hacker, figures out that suspicious nodes are in place in certain Internet servers which have the capability to disrupt the entire Internet. He would soon call Chloe and report his findings, inadvertently leading terrorists to his door.

Audrey Raines, overcome with emotion, tries to comfort her father, Secretary of Defense James Heller, after terrorists took them prisoner. Heller counsels his daughter to look for an opportunity to escape once the terrorists begin staging a show trial for him, to be broadcast on the Internet.

09:42AM

07:00AM

A train explodes in the Santa Clarita Valley as part of a strategic attack to allow an operative named Dar to steal the Dobson Override Device from a courier and then deliver it to Habib Marwan's organization.

07:25AM

On orders from his new boss, Secretary of Defense James Heller, Jack Bauer—retired from the field—returns to CTU to discuss it's budgeting process, and to learn more about the agency's investigation of the train bombing.

07:58AM

Secretary of Defense James Heller and his daughter, Audrey Raines, are boldly abducted in broad daylight by men working for the terrorist cell run by a man known only as Omar.

08:58AM

Terrorists broadcast a live-stream video over the Internet of a bound Defense Secretary James Heller as he is about to be put on trial and then executed in front of the whole world.

09:35AM	10:40AM	12:05PM	12:08PM

Jack Bauer aims a sniper rifle at two thugs working for terrorist Kalil Hasan seconds before they kill computer hacker Andrew Paige, a friend of Chloe O'Brian's. He saved Paige, and then resumed his pursuit of Hasan.	Behrooz Araz watches his girlfriend, Debbie, die after being poisoned by his mother, Dina. Debbie had inadvertently compromised the Araz family's role as a secret terror cell working for Habib Marwan.	Audrey Raines spots Jack Bauer from her cell in the underground compound where she and her father are imprisoned. Bauer promises to return for her after he has found her father.	Led by Jack Bauer, a U.S. Marine Special Forces assault unit rappels from a Cobra attack helicopter as part of an attack mounted to rescue James Heller and Audrey Raines.

SECRET CELL

Nuclear disaster seems imminent, and relationships begin to shatter. Edgar Stiles heroically programs a method for shutting down the impacted nuclear facilities, but tragically, one reactor continues melting down, killing, among others, Edgar's mother. On the other side, the Araz family is faring no better. The fanatical Navi Araz agrees to Habib Marwan's demand that he kill his own son, Behrooz, after learning of the boy's involvement with an American girl, but his wife, Dina, chooses to help the boy, and the two of them flee. When Jack Bauer prevents Navi from killing Behrooz, the boy shoots his father dead. Bauer and Audrey Raines, meanwhile, are ambushed while pursuing evidence about Marwan, and then saved only because Bauer called in former colleague Tony Almeida. Despite his fall from grace, Almeida decides to help CTU, but just as he is settling in his former wife, Michelle Dessler, returns to command CTU and complicate his life. Simultaneously, when Bauer pursues evidence that Audrey's estranged husband, Paul Raines, may be connected to the day's events, Bauer reveals a brutal side to his character, and their relationship becomes strained.

11:44AM

01:55PM

Tony Almeida shows up to the Felsted Security facility in time to save Jack Bauer and Audrey Raines from thugs closing in on them. Bauer and Raines were seeking security camera footage to help identify Habib Marwan.

01:57PM

Edgar Stiles methodically works through a sequence of computer commands designed to break the Dobson Override's control of 17 nuclear power plants. Stiles managed to halt meltdowns at 16 of the 17 facilities.

02:46PM

Behrooz and Dina Araz escape from a medical clinic where she was being treated for a gunshot wound inflicted by her husband. Behrooz realizes officials at the clinic are calling the authorities.

03:16PM

Television reports cover the meltdown of the San Gabriel Island nuclear reactor—the only facility Edgar Stiles was unable to save. Ironically, fallout from the meltdown killed Edgar's mother, among thousands of others.

Navi Araz, leader of a sleeper cell consisting of his seemingly normal family, consults by phone with Omar about the death of Kalil Hasan. While he talked, Araz's wife, Dina, and son, Behrooz, were preparing to dispose of the body of Debbie Pendleton, Behrooz's girlfriend, murdered earlier by Dina. Navi was so concerned about his wife and son complicating the Day 4 terror plot that he later tried to have them both killed for disobeying him.

PRIME SUSPECTS

Habib Marwan

Marwan was the leader of a terror organization called Turkish Crimson Jihad who cultivated secret terror cells inside the United States. On Day 4, he masterminded a series of major attacks before Jack Bauer finally caught up to him. Marwan then killed himself rather than allow himself to be interrogated.

SLEEPER CELLS

Sleeper cells are small groups of terrorists that attempt to blend into their surroundings and operate undercover until such time as they are "activated" by their handlers. Members usually know each other, but often do not know members of other cells, or even their superiors. This is done to maintain secrecy and limit the ability for one cell to incriminate any others in the event of capture by the authorities. On Day 4, the Araz family was activated. They were a perfect sleeper cell in that they completely blended into their suburban surroundings until it was time for them to act.

04:03PM

Avi Naraz confronts his son, Behrooz, in the laundry room at Lindauer Memorial Hospital. Avi planned to kill his son, but Jack arrived and saved the boy. Behrooz then shot and killed his father.

05:00PM

Jack Bauer, suspicious of Paul Raines' connection to the theft of the Dobson Override Device, plans to torture Raines for information in front of a horrified Audrey Raines—Paul's estranged wife.

06:57PM

Lights in buildings across LA begin to go out as the EMP bomb at McLennan-Forster is activated to prevent CTU from linking the company to the day's events. The device destroyed electronic circuitry for several miles.

06:59PM

Michelle Dessler returns to CTU to take over as Special Agent in Charge from her ex-husband, Tony Almeida, who managed the unit after Erin Driscoll was forced to step down due to the death of her daughter.

MARWAN'S PLAN

Corrupt officials at defense contractor McLennan-Forster detonate an Electromagnetic Pulse bomb (EMP) to misdirect CTU's investigation, and attempt to kill Jack Bauer and Paul Raines. Raines is seriously wounded when he takes a bullet intended for Bauer. Jack next forces Dina Araz to lead him to Habib Marwan—she is killed, but CTU saves Bauer, and he leads an assault that just misses Marwan. The terrorist then pursues his plan's next phase—the theft of a Stealth fighter and shoot-down of Air Force One. When two civilians find the so-called "Nuclear Football" at the crash site, Bauer saves them from Marwan and gets the football back, but not before Marwan escapes with crucial launch and location codes. Marwan's agenda becomes clear when his men next steal a nuclear warhead—he plans a devastating missile attack inside the United States.

STEALTH FIGHTER

The top-secret plane stolen on Day 4 by Mitch Anderson and used to shoot down Air Force One was the F-117A Nighthawk—a key weapon used by the United States Air Force. The Nighthawk is specifically designed to avoid radar detection in order to penetrate tight air defenses and attack targets of high value at night. It does not carry radar itself, because that would increase the ability of other systems to detect it. Instead, it navigates by integrating GPS and high-accuracy inertial systems. It is primarily a ground attack aircraft, carries laser-guided weapons and surface-to-air missiles, and is always manned by just a single pilot.

McLennan-Forster's electromagnetic pulse bomb (EMP) gets powered up seconds before Jack Bauer enters the room. Bauer managed to partially close the safety chamber, but his effort wasn't enough—the device's electromagnetic shockwave destroyed electrical circuitry within several miles of the blast site.

07:58PM

Paul Raines pushes Bauer out of the way and takes a bullet intended for Jack. McLennan-Forster official Dave Conlon fired the shot, and Bauer killed him seconds later. Raines was severely wounded, and rushed to CTU.

08:58PM

Dina Araz aims a gun at Jack Bauer's head on orders from Habib Marwan. Desperate to save her son, she instead tries to shoot Marwan, but the gun is empty. Moments later Marwan has her killed.

09:33PM

Michelle Dessler introduces Bill Buchanan to the CTU staff for the first time. Buchanan came to CTU Los Angeles from Division command to oversee the exchange of Behrooz Araz for Jack Bauer.

09:59PM

Mitch Anderson, posing as an Air Force pilot, taxis on the runway for takeoff in a F-117A Nighthawk Stealth Fighter jet, stolen as part of Marwan's plan to kill President Keeler.

FAMILY TRAGEDY

CTU Special Agent in Charge Erin Driscoll tries calming her schizophrenic daughter, Maya, in the CTU medical clinic. Maya was involved in an incident that forced Driscoll to bring her to CTU for monitoring while Day 4 unfolded. But Maya committed suicide by slitting her wrists, forcing Driscoll to step down and hand over authority to Tony Almeida.

PRIME SUSPECT

Mitch Anderson

Anderson was a dishonorably discharged and briefly imprisoned military officer who later became the mercenary who implemented Habib Marwan's plan to steal a Stealth Fighter and shoot down Air Force One. He was then shot down himself and apparently killed, but his body was never found.

Charles Logan became president when terrorist Mitch Anderson shot down Air Force One. President John Keeler wasn't killed, but was severely injured, leading to Logan's ascension under the 25th Amendment.

NUCLEAR FOOTBALL

The term "Nuclear Football" refers to a briefcase that is carried everywhere the President of the United States goes in the event he should need to order a massive nuclear attack. It contains daily changed nuclear launch codes and a "playbook" of so-called Gold Codes that illustrate various options for attack scenarios, as well as nuclear warhead location information. On Day 4, Habib Marwan did not steal the entire nuclear football, but he did manage to take pages that included warhead activation codes matching the warhead his organization stole in Iowa, giving him tremendous power.

10:42 PM

Bauer pumps rounds through a wall to kill an assassin named Nicole at Mitch Anderson's apartment. Nicole helped Anderson steal an Air Force pilot's identity, and her next assignment was to stop Bauer.

10:59 AM

Radar shows Air Force One, carrying President John Keeler, suffering an indirect hit from a missile fired from the stolen Stealth Fighter jet. He was injured in the attack, and replaced by Vice President Charles Logan.

11:45 PM

Habib Marwan acquires parts of the Nuclear Football playbook, which contains American nuclear warhead locations and activation codes, after taking it from a civilian who found it in the wreckage of Air Force One.

12:59 AM

To learn Marwan's location, Bauer roughs up Joe Prado, a middleman who helped Marwan smuggle people out of the country. Marwan sends Prado, a lawyer, to delay his interview, but Bauer broke protocol to get the information.

ENDGAME

Acting President Logan allows former President David Palmer to coordinate operations, and Palmer sanctions a plan to invade the Chinese Consulate and capture a rogue scientist connected to Marwan. The raid goes bad, and the scientist is wounded, so Bauer forces a surgeon to save the scientist while Paul Raines dies on the operating table. The lead he gives them is then wasted when Logan interferes with a move on Marwan. When the mercenary Mandy is captured after taking Tony Almeida hostage, however, CTU finally gets Marwan's location from her, in return for a presidential pardon. After the missile is launched, Marwan kills himself, but CTU finds data that averts disaster. However, that isn't the end as the Chinese demand custody of Bauer, causing elements inside the U.S. government to plan his assassination. To save himself, Bauer fakes his own death. With only Almeida, Michelle Dessler, Chloe O'Brian, and Palmer knowing the truth, Bauer quietly disappears.

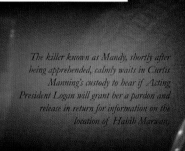

The killer known as Mandy, shortly after being apprehended, calmly waits in Curtis Manning's custody to hear if Acting President Logan will grant her a pardon and release in return for information on the location of Habib Marwan.

`01:38AM`

Former President David Palmer takes a call from Mike Novick, asking him to come to the White House immediately to advise Acting President Charles Logan on how to handle the growing crisis.

`01:59AM`

Chloe O'Brian, on her first field assignment, fires at a gunman trying to stop her for harvesting important data relating to the terror plot from Sabir Ardakani's computer. O'Brian saved herself and Ardakani's girlfriend, Nabilla.

`02:31AM`

A masked Jack Bauer illegally enters the Chinese Consulate, guided by Tony Almeida via radio, in search of scientist Lee Jong, who may possess crucial information about Marwan's plan to launch a nuclear warhead.

`02:57AM`

Jack Bauer tries, and fails, to resuscitate Paul Raines, who dies on the operating table at CTU. Bauer ordered Raines' surgeon to abandon him to work on saving Lee Jong in hopes of learning clues about Marwan's location.

CONSULATE INTEGRITY

Jack Bauer's invasion of the Chinese Consulate was an extremely serious matter because, according to international law, he was attacking a foreign nation. Like embassies, consulates are considered home territory of the nation operating them. They generally function as business offices in various overseas locations—issuing passports and visas, and aiding the business and legal interests of citizens living abroad. Since they are considered foreign property, they can only be entered upon invitation of the country running the consulate.

05:56AM

PRIME SUSPECTS

MANDY

Mandy is a mercenary assassin working for terror networks. She surfaced on Day 4 to help Habib Marwan arrange the James Heller kidnapping, and later took Tony Almeida hostage while trying to escape. Jack Bauer stopped her, but she negotiated a pardon, gave up Marwan's location, and then disappeared.

SIMULATING DEATH

Jack Bauer's plan to simulate his death involved the use of so-called "beta blocker" drugs to reduce his heart rate to a virtually undetectable level. Such drugs are normally used to reduce stress on the heart and prevent angina attacks, or to slow down abnormally fast heart rhythms. Overuse of the drugs can stop the heart, and at the end of Day 4, Bauer used them far past their intended application. Fortunately, a shot of epinephrine, administered by Tony Almeida, restored his heart rate before a fatal episode could occur. Epinephrine is normally used on patients suffering from cardiac arrest to restore a heart beat.

03:11AM

Habib Marwan's men configure a cruise missile to carry the modified nuclear warhead. Shortly after, the deadly nuclear missile is launched from a mobile launching site in Iowa.

06:09AM

Jack Bauer struggles to pull Habib Marwan to safety after the terrorist tried to jump to his death, rather than be interrogated. But Marwan used his knife to slash Bauer's hand, forcing him to drop Marwan.

06:22AM

A radar image displayed on screens at CTU show an F-18 successfully shooting down the cruise missile carrying the nuclear warhead, just moments before it can strike Los Angeles.

06:53AM

Tony Almeida, Chloe O'Brian, and Michelle Dessler wait to see if a shot of epinephrine will revive Jack Bauer after he faked his death to thwart an attempt on his life. For a few anxious seconds, it wasn't clear if he would survive.

DAY 5

18 months later …

As Day 5 gets underway, Wayne Palmer cradles his brother, former President David Palmer, seconds after David was shot dead. David Palmer and the other people who knew Jack Bauer was still alive were targeted for death on Day 5, with only Chloe O'Brian surviving. Those events forced Bauer out of hiding and into a race to help CTU stop a nerve gas terror plot and a government conspiracy reaching all the way into the White House of President Charles Logan.

CONSPIRACY

The conspiracy unfolds in gut-wrenching fashion with David Palmer's assassination. Michelle Dessler's murder follows, along with attacks on Tony Almeida and Chloe O'Brian. CTU finds manufactured evidence framing Jack Bauer—long believed dead. Chloe summons Bauer out of hiding, and he saves her life before uncovering information that leads him to Ontario Airport. There, he encounters a hostage crisis supposedly designed to stop President Logan's treaty with Russia. In reality, the attack was a ruse to help terrorists steal deadly nerve gas and smuggle it into Asia in a strategy to increase American regional influence. First Lady Martha Logan also suspects a conspiracy, but is outmaneuvered by Logan's aide, Walt Cummings, a key player in the plot. Bauer finally returns to CTU, finds a link to Cummings, and confronts him in front of the President. But Logan has another agenda, and pulls Bauer deeper into the conspiracy.

09:08AM

07:02AM	07:13AM	07:52AM	08:00AM

Former President David Palmer lies dead on the floor of Wayne Palmer's high-rise apartment, seconds after he was assassinated with a bullet to the neck. The killing launched a far-reaching conspiracy on Day 5.	*Tony Almeida is knocked to the floor as the explosion that killed his wife, Michelle Dessler, blows out windows in his home. Seconds later, Almeida would rush to Dessler's side and be severely injured himself.*	*Jack Bauer calms Chloe O'Brian when they reunite at an oil refinery as Chloe flees for her life. Soon after, the killer who murdered David Palmer would show up hunting Chloe, only to lose a confrontation with Bauer.*	*CTU operative, Edgar Stiles plays back security camera footage that appears to implicate the supposedly dead Jack Bauer as the assassin who shot ex President David Palmer.*

President Charles Logan and Russian President Yuri Suvarov greet the media after Suvarov arrives at Logan's retreat to sign a comprehensive anti-terrorism treaty.

NERVE GAS

Terrorists used canisters of weaponized Sentox VX-1 nerve gas, manufactured by Omicron International and triggered with remote devices like the one pictured here, on Day 5. The remote device featured twin USB plug-in ports to download triggering codes, and then transmitted those codes to the canister's locked trigger mechanism using wireless technology. VX is the most deadly form of nerve gas—so named because it attacks the nervous system and quickly causes respiratory failure and death.

PRIME SUSPECTS

Haas

Haas, an assassin was hired by disgraced ex CTU Special Agent in Charge, Christopher Henderson, to kill David Palmer, Michelle Dessler, Tony Almeida, and Chloe O'Brian. Bauer captured Haas early on Day 5, and shot him to death.

James Nathanson

Nathanson was a former CIA officer serving the Day 5 conspiracy out of a misguided sense of patriotism. He acted as a middleman in the nerve gas plot, but later turned on the plan, and was killed by his co-conspirators.

09:58ᴀᴍ	10:58ᴀᴍ	11:28ᴀᴍ	12:44ᴘᴍ

To save Derek Huxley, Jack surrenders to Anton Beresch at the Ontario Airport and becomes a fellow hostage. Beresch wanted to prevent the signing of an anti-terrorism treaty between the U.S. and Russia.

President Logan's Chief of Staff Walt Cummings chloroforms First Lady Martha Logan and steals evidence which proves her claim that an audio recording of the late David Palmer was doctored.

Jack Bauer returns to CTU after the airport hostage crisis, shocking most of the staff who thought he was dead. Acting Special Agent in Charge, Lynn McGill asks Jack to help CTU grapple with the nerve gas plot.

Bauer confronts Cummings in front of President Logan about his involvement in the deaths of David Palmer and others. Bauer did not yet realize that Logan was manipulating Cummings as part of a larger plot.

CORRUPTION

Terrorists attack with nerve gas at a mall and hospital, where only CTU's heroic work prevents disasters. They also try to kill the Russian President with President Logan's apparent acceptance. But Martha Logan endangers herself to save the Suvarovs, with help from Secret Service Agent Aaron Pierce. When Walt Cummings dies under mysterious circumstances, and she learns of her husband's acquiescence to terrorists, Martha uncovers his administration's links to the conspiracy. Jack Bauer, meanwhile, discovers that his former mentor at CTU, Christopher Henderson, may be connected to the nerve gas plot, and when he investigates, Henderson tries to kill him. Bauer survives, and captures Henderson, taking him to CTU for interrogation. But before CTU can break Henderson, terrorists stage a deadly nerve gas attack on the agency—killing dozens, including Edgar Stiles and Lynn McGill, and grinding CTU to a halt.

01:45am

TRUTH SERUMS

CTU used the drug Hyoscine-Pentothal to force Christopher Henderson to talk. It's a form of a so-called "truth drug," designed to impair judgment in the subject, making it difficult for that person to conceal the truth, and to cause pain, when necessary. The best-known truth drug is Sodium Pentothal, and Hyoscine-Pentothal is similar to that. Such drugs are intravenous sedatives, usually injected in small doses, but they are not foolproof. Indeed, Henderson was able to resist the drugs and refused to give CTU any information.

02:45pm

Jack Bauer rushes a little girl out of the Sunrise Hills Mall to safety after terrorists released nerve gas into the ventilation system. Bauer shut down the flow of gas before a full-scale tragedy could occur, but 11 people died.

03:58pm

Martha Logan gets into the car carrying Russian President Yuri Suvarov and his wife. She knew terrorists were targeting Suvarov, and when her husband wouldn't warn them, Martha got into the vehicle to force his hand.

04:47pm

The Suvarov's motorcade comes under attack as Vladimir Bierko's men fire a missile at his car. Secret Service Agent Aaron Pierce ordered the car to be turned around, which saved it from taking a direct hit.

05:46pm

At the Thomas Memorial Hospital, Curtis Manning catches terrorist Viktor Grigorin setting a timer to release nerve gas. Manning killed Grigorin and got the gas canister into an isolation chamber just before it detonated.

Audrey Raines aims a gun at the man responsible for her suffering—Christopher Henderson—planning to shoot him before his men arrive. She couldn't do it, however, and was later saved by CTU agent, Curtis Manning.

PRIME SUSPECTS

Walt Cummings

Cummings, President Logan's Chief of Staff, was driven by a warped patriotism to give terrorists access to nerve gas, thinking they would be caught using it in Russia. He was exposed and later found dead after a presumed suicide, but it's more likely he was murdered.

Vladimir Bierko

Bierko, a financier of Russian radicals, stole nerve gas to use against Russia, but CTU interfered, so he attacked U.S. targets instead. Jack Bauer halted an attack and captured Bierko, but he later escaped and tried another strike. Bauer then killed him in a fist fight.

05:56PM	06:26PM	06:54PM	06:59PM

Trying to force Christopher Henderson to provide information about the nerve gas, Jack Bauer shoots Henderson's wife, Miriam, in the leg. In spite of this Henderson still refused to talk.

Christopher Henderson is taken to CTU where he is tortured using Hyoscine-Pentothal. He is warned it will get more painful unless he talks. Agent Burke gave him a second dose, but Henderson still refused to talk.

Edgar Stiles discovers Carrie Bendis' dead body in an electrical room after the terrorist Ostroff killed her while planting a nerve gas canister in the CTU ventilation system. Moments later, the gas would claim Edgar's life.

Chloe O'Brien watches in horror through a sealed door in the CTU Situation Room as her friend and colleague, Edgar Stiles, dies from Sentox Nerve Gas poisoning after failing to get to a safe room in time.

HEROIC MEASURES

As CTU reels, tragedy strikes again—Christopher Henderson murders Tony Almeida and escapes, while Jack Bauer pursues Vladimir Bierko. After being sidetracked into suspecting Audrey Raines, he prevents a cataclysmic terror attack and finally captures Bierko. President Logan, however, reveals himself to be orchestrating the day's events in concert with a secret group that includes a mysterious man named Graem. With Henderson's help, Logan scrambles to cover up his role, and orders the Department of Homeland Security to absorb CTU. Bauer seeks an audio recording implicating President Logan, barely beats Henderson to the evidence, and plays the recording for Secretary of Defense James Heller, who tries to force Logan's resignation. Just as Logan is ready to capitulate, Henderson makes Bauer exchange the evidence for Raines' life, and Logan moves a step closer to eliminating proof of his misdeeds.

07:43PM

Lynn McGill dies after heroically sacrificing his life to fix a computer program controlling CTU's ventilation system. This allowed the facility to be flushed of toxic gas, saving those still alive in the building.

07:58PM

Tony Almeida lies dead on the floor of CTU's medical clinic after Christopher Henderson stabbed him with a Hyoscine-Pentothal syringe. Almeida had hesitated when he had a chance to kill Henderson, and it cost him his life.

08:58PM

Collette Stenger, an information broker working for Henderson, finally gives Bauer the location of Bierko's safe house. Whilst being interrogated she implicates Audrey Raines, insisting she obtained information from her.

09:57PM

Bauer races out of the Wilshire Gas Company facility as it explodes. He set explosives to destroy the building, and with it, the Sentox nerve gas that Bierko released into natural gas pipes, saving many thousands of lives.

Jack Bauer and Christopher Henderson infiltrate a Russian submarine to stop Vladimir Bierko. Henderson later tried to slip away from Bauer, but Bauer gave him an unloaded gun, and later killed him.

05:08AM

PRIME SUSPECTS

Christopher Henderson

Henderson was a former CTU official who mentored Jack Bauer, until Bauer implicated him in a scandal. He went into private business, but joined the Day 5 conspiracy, doing President Logan's dirty work.

Graem

Graem led a private group of businessmen who masterminded the Day 5 conspiracy with President Logan in order to control Asian oil assets. When Logan went down, Graem quietly disappeared, and it wasn't until Day 6 that it became clear he was Jack Bauer's brother.

10:05PM

Karen Hayes and her aide, Miles Papazian, confer about possibly using Audrey Raines to connect Bill Buchanan to CTU's security woes on Day 5, as a way of forcing him to step aside quietly.

10:41PM

Jack Bauer, Wayne Palmer, and Evelyn Martin confer about locating the recording incriminating Logan in the day's events. Martin agrees to point Bauer to the missing recording if he helps rescue her daughter from Henderson.

11:06PM

For the first time President Logan is shown to be directly involved in Day 5's manipulations when he takes a secret call from Henderson who promises to kill Jack Bauer and Wayne Palmer, and suppress evidence against Logan.

12:41AM

Secretary of Defense James Heller confronts President Logan after hearing the audio recording located by Bauer. He demands Logan resign in return for keeping the information from law enforcement agencies and the media.

A PRESIDENT FALLS

While President Logan pursues his enemies, Jack Bauer corners Christopher Henderson, only to learn Henderson has passed the incriminating recording to a courier. Henderson almost murders Audrey Raines and escapes, but Curtis Manning stops him. Bauer next hijacks a diplomatic plane carrying Henderson's courier, and recovers the recording, but Homeland Security official Miles Papazian destroys it at Logan's behest. Bauer then chases Vladimir Bierko after he escapes and seizes a Russian submarine. Henderson helps Bauer stop Bierko, and kill him, in return for a helping him disappear, but when Henderson betrays Bauer, Jack shoots him dead. Bauer fails to force a confession from Logan, but does plant a listening device on him. When Martha Logan enrages the President, CTU records him angrily admitting his guilt. After eulogizing David Palmer, Logan is arrested for treason, while Bauer reunites with Audrey Raines. But Chinese agents snatch Bauer as payback for Day 4 events, and as Day 5 fades, a beaten Jack Bauer heads into the darkness of a Chinese prison.

Martha Logan coldly meets her husband's gaze as security official escort President Logan from David Palmer's tribute service. Martha played a central role in bringing him down.

James Heller intentionally drives his car off a cliff to prevent Christopher Henderson from using his life as a bargaining chip to force Jack Bauer to let him go. Heller ended up surviving the crash.

Graem, a mysterious man who would later turn out to be Jack Bauer's brother, speaks to President Logan about ensuring his wife, Martha Logan, does not expose them. It's the first moment Logan's co-conspirators are revealed.

Jack Bauer breaks into the cockpit of a diplomatic plane he has hijacked to force the co-pilot, Scott Evans, to hand over the audio recording implicating President Logan. Bauer then made Evans land the plane on a freeway.

Vladimir Bierko drops a Sentox nerve gas canister into the Russian submarine Natalia. He killed the crew, and was trying to fire the sub's missiles into Los Angeles when Jack Bauer caught up to him, and killed him.

Charles Logan

Logan insisted he was acting in America's interest when he joined a conspiracy to help terrorists acquire nerve gas. But he showed that he was only too willing to violently cover up events like David Palmer's murder. On Day 5 Logan became the most criminal senior official in U.S. history.

Cheng Zhi

On Day 4, Cheng Zhi served as head of security at the Chinese Consulate in Los Angeles, but may well have had a more senior position. After discovering Jack Bauer was not dead on Day 5, he kidnapped him to extract American intelligence secrets.

05:20AM	06:19AM	06:32AM	06:57AM

After dealing with Vladimir Bierko, Jack Bauer shoots and kills Christopher Henderson after his former mentor pulled a gun on him while trying to escape.

Bauer abducts and questions President Logan about his role in the conspiracy and threatens to kill him, but can't get a confession. He does plant a microphone transmitter on Logan however, which is later used to prove his guilt.

President Logan slaps Martha Logan, accusing her of helping Jack Bauer. During the ensuing argument, Logan admits his role in the conspiracy, and is recorded by the transmitter planted by Bauer.

A badly beaten Jack Bauer lies barely alive inside the hold of a cargo ship bound for China, after Chinese intelligence officials abducted him as Day 5 comes to an end.

20 months later …

Amushroom cloud over suburban Los Angeles: A worst-case scenario comes true early on Day 6 as terrorists detonate a nuclear device. Thia act awakens Jack Bauer—newly freed after almost two years in a Chinese military prison—from his revulsion at returning to his former life. It sends him on a desperate journey that exposes the involvement of his own father and brother in the day's tragic events—events that threaten to escalate into a global war.

THE NIGHTMARE

Jack returns from a Chinese military prison, only to be handed to terrorist Abu Fayed in return for information on Hamri Al-Assad—the man believed to be responsible for an 11-week terror wave on US soil. However, Fayed is the real mastermind. He tortures Bauer, but Jack manages to escape, locate Al-Assad, and prevent a suicide bombing. But Fayed acquires a triggering mechanism for one of several stolen Russian suitcase nukes and plans to activate the bomb. Meanwhile, President Wayne Palmer's desperate administration detains Muslims across the nation—leading the President into conflict with his sister, Sandra. Palmer grants Al-Assad a pardon to help locate Fayed, and that pushes Bauer into a bloody confrontation with his friend, Curtis Manning. After Manning's death, a distraught Bauer appears unable to continue. But when Fayed detonates a nuke, killing thousands of Americans—Bauer summons the determination to hunt those responsible.

06:08am	06:54am	07:15am	07:54am

After holding him prisoner for over 20 months, Chinese officials turn a shackled Jack Bauer over to CTU representatives at Ellis Airfield early on Day 6—as part of a deal brokered by President Wayne Palmer.	*After brutally torturing Jack (revenge for Jack's torture of Fayed's brother), Abu Fayed confesses that he is behind the wave of violent attacks across the nation, not the man CTU suspects—Hamri Al-Assad.*	*After locating Hamri Al-Assad, Jack Bauer leads him and an injured terrorist suspected of collaborating with Abu Fayed out of a safe house—seconds before it is destroyed by a precision air strike.*	*As he battles Jack Bauer, a suicide bomber named Nasir attempts to detonate C-4 explosives on a Los Angeles subway car. Bauer knocked him out of the car before the detonation, saving dozens of lives.*

PRIME SUSPECTS

ABU FAYED

Fayed is the most prolific mass murderer Jack Bauer has ever faced, having detonated a nuclear weapon that killed over 12,000 people on Day 6. Bauer relentlessly hunted Fayed, and killed him in a brutal fistfight.

AHMED AMAR

Teenager Amar's father was suspected of collaborating with terrorists. Ahmed was the real collaborator, and on Day 6 he forced a neighbor to deliver a nuclear component to Fayed. Jack Bauer later shot Amar dead.

A distraught Jack Bauer drops his gun, after reluctantly firing the shot that killed CTU agent, Curtis Manning. The terrible act saved a known terrorist, Hamri Al-Assad— the vital source in CTU's race to find missing nuclear weapons.

SUITCASE NUKES

Five suitcase nuclear devices were relics from the Cold War, targeted for destruction when Russian nationalist Dimitri Gredenko supplied them to terrorists. The devices are so named because the warhead and firing mechanism are small enough to fit into a briefcase. They were developed by the Soviet Union in the 1960s and their internal components included FB sub-circuit boards that contained encrypted Russian security codes. After terrorists detonated one of the bombs in California on Day 6, the theft of one of those boards precipitated a second crisis.

Although the triggering device for the suitcase nukes was built out of regular computer components, it required a highly trained engineer to program it.

09:55am

Moments after killing Curtis Manning, Bauer reaches a low point, uncertain whether he has the strength or the desire to continue the fight. Manning had been about to kill Al-Assad, but Jack needed the terrorist alive.

10:09am

After the nearby nuclear explosion, Jack races to rescue a helicopter pilot trapped on the roof of a building. The copter was buffeted by the explosion's shockwave, and blown into the building.

11:06am

Jack interrogates his brother, Graem, after learning of Graem and his father's connection to Gredenko—the man who helped terrorists acquire nuclear weapons. At first Graem tried to mislead his brother.

11:34am

Phillip Bauer surprises his estranged son, Jack, at Enegra Global, the defense contracting firm that employed Darren McCarthy—a consultant hired by Phillip who illegally trafficked Russian nuclear weapons.

FAMILY MATTERS

When Jack Bauer discovers his family's connection to the missing nuclear weapons, he confronts his estranged brother, Graem, and their father, Phillip. Phillip convinces Jack that only Graem was involved, so Jack brutally interrogates his brother and learns, to his horror, that Graem ran the Day 5 conspiracy. Meanwhile, CTU's Morris O'Brian is kidnapped and forced to program another nuclear weapon trigger device, while Abu Fayed conspires with Dimitri Gredenko to launch more attacks. When CTU goes after Gredenko, Phillip Bauer—afraid Jack will learn of his connection to Gredenko—murders Graem, tries to kill Jack, and kidnaps his grandson, Josh. Jack confronts Phillip, rescues Josh, and learns that former President Charles Logan also has links to Gredenko. At the same time, extremists inside the government try to kill President Palmer.

Phillip Bauer brings his confused grandson, Josh, to a hotel. He confronts the boy and makes it clear that he is not to interfere with his plans, or try to slip away.

12:58PM	01:48PM	01:56PM	02:59PM

Phillip Bauer administers a massive dose of Hyoscine-Pentothal to kill his son, Graem. He is desperate to prevent Graem from revealing his company's role in the terror plot during his interrogation by CTU.

Under duress, Morris O'Brian completes programming a nuclear bomb trigger device for Abu Fayed. Fayed planned to kill O'Brian moments later, but a CTU TAC team saved him just in time.

Jack carefully follows Chloe O'Brian's instructions to disarm a suitcase nuke left by Abu Fayed shortly before CTU rescued Morris O'Brian. Bauer managed the task successfully, preventing an epic disaster.

CTU agent, Milo Pressman detonates a CTU tactical van in order to allow himself and Marilyn Bauer time to escape thugs working for Phillip Bauer who had ambushed the CTU team.

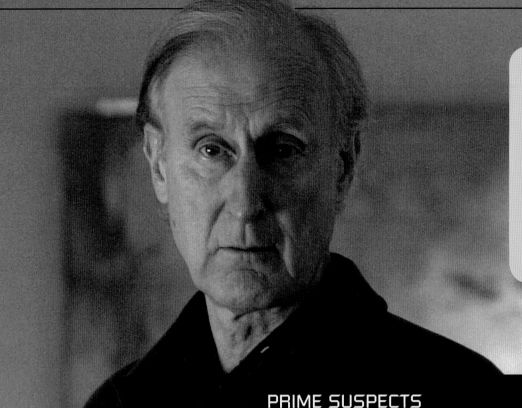

INTERROGATION

When his brother pushed his interrogation past safe limits on Day 6 Graem Bauer tolerated extreme levels of the truth drug, Hyoscine-Pentothal. At Jack's insistence, Agent Burke administered 8cc of the drug before Graem confessed to his role in the Day 5 murders of David Palmer, Tony Almeida, and Michelle Dessler. But even then, he did not reveal his father's company's involvement in the developing nuclear crisis. Finally, Burke refused to administer a higher dose. However, Phillip Bauer knew that Graem would not be able to resist indefinitely, so he used the drug to kill his youngest son and guarantee his silence.

PRIME SUSPECTS

Graem Bauer
Dimitri Gredenko used Graem and Phillip Bauer's connection to the Day 5 plot to blackmail them into helping him steal the nuclear devices. Jack Bauer used brutal interrogation methods to make his brother talk, but ultimately it was their father who silenced Graem permanently.

Dimitri Gredenko
Gredenko was a former Russian general and nationalist who aided the nuclear bomb plot in order to force the United States and Arab countries into conflict. In the end, Gredenko was captured, forced to set up Abu Fayed, and later died trying to escape.

Darren McCarthy
Phillip Bauer hired McCarthy to supervise the dismantling of Russian nukes, but he sold them to terrorists instead. For more money, McCarthy kidnapped Morris O'Brian to help program the devices. But McCarthy's girlfriend later murdered him to grab the payday for herself.

 **03:38PM**   **03:59PM**   **04:59PM**   **05:47PM**

Reed Pollock assaults Tom Lennox in the boiler room of the Presidential bunker when he realizes Lennox will expose his plan to murder President Wayne Palmer. Pollock detained Lennox while the plot was executed.

A PDA left behind by Phillip Bauer gives Jack an important clue in his search for missing Russian nuclear weapons—a private phone number for a man linked to Dimitri Gredenko, former President Charles Logan.

As Al-Assad begins a speech rejecting terrorism, he discovers a bomb on the podium. He puts himself between the bomb and the President—Palmer survives, albeit in a coma, but Al-Assad is killed instantly.

Jack threatens to shoot Russian diplomat Anatoly Markov to get Dimitri Gredenko's location. Markov finally admitted Gredenko was operating in the Mojave Desert, but sneered that Bauer was too late to stop him.

HUNTING FAYED

With President Palmer unconscious and Vice President Noah Daniels in control, Jack Bauer takes drastic measures to locate Dimitri Gredenko. An unstable Martha Logan attacks her former husband, Charles Logan, when he seeks her help in getting Russian cooperation with CTU. Gredenko and Abu Fayed attempt a nuclear attack on San Francisco, but CTU interferes, captures Gredenko, and uses him to find Fayed, who CTU hopes will lead them to the nuclear devices. Meanwhile, Daniels prepares a major retaliatory attack, so Sandra Palmer has President Palmer revived to stop him. Palmer does so, but then tries a risky gamble to help CTU. It works—Bauer locates the nukes and kills Fayed. However, Palmer then collapses from a cerebral hemorrhage, while Bauer learns that Audrey Raines is alive in Chinese custody. The price of her freedom is a bomb component that could compromise Russian security.

Jack Bauer accompanies former President Charles Logan from his private retreat, where he has been under house arrest for almost two years. They are heading to the Russian Consulate to convince diplomat Anatoly Markov to help them locate Dimitri Gredenko.

| 06:03PM | 06:33PM | 07:02PM | 07:54PM |

Bill Buchanan introduces Mike Doyle as the new CTU Director of Field Operations to take charge of an assault on the Russian Consulate, where Jack is being held with knowledge of Gredenko's nuclear strike plans.

Martha Logan gives her former husband an icy greeting when they reunite at her home. Logan wanted Martha to help convince the Russian government to assist CTU, but she brutally attacked him a short time later.

An unmanned RQ-2 series Unmanned Aerial Vehicle (UAV), or aerial drone, armed with a nuclear bomb by Dimitri Gredenko and Abu Fayed, takes off from the Mojave Desert, targeting San Francisco.

Jack Bauer struggles to use a remote flight control system to steer the aerial drone aimed at San Francisco away from its target. Bauer managed to crash land the vehicle, which leaked radiation, but did not detonate.

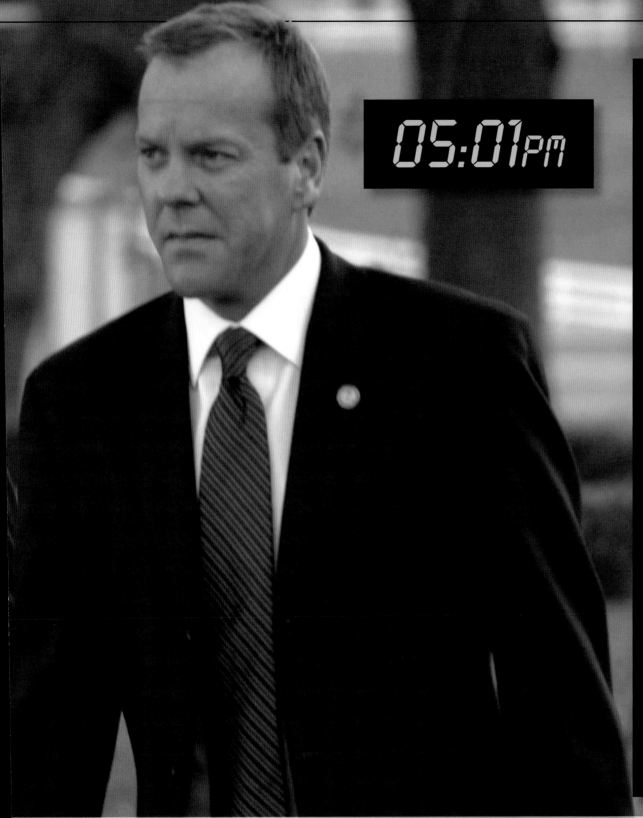

05:01pm

REED POLLOCK

Pollock was Deputy Chief of Staff, serving under Tom Lennox, and secretly an extremist opposed to Wayne Palmer's foreign policy. Insisting he was a patriot, Pollock ran the plot to kill Palmer, and placed the bomb himself. As Day 6 ended, he was in custody.

BRUCE CARSON

Carson was a security specialist and Reed Pollock's ally in the Wayne Palmer assassination plot. With Pollock's help, he snuck liquid bomb components into the Presidential Bunker and built the bomb. Tom Lennox turned in both Carson and Pollock.

07:57pm

Noah Daniels orders the military to proceed with a nuclear strike in the Middle East, against the advice of his top advisors. Daniels considered the foiled attack on San Francisco sufficient justification for this order.

08:58pm

After awakening from his medically induced coma, President Wayne Palmer, calls Vice President Daniels to explain he has canceled plans for the nuclear attack in the Middle East and is resuming his duties.

10:56pm

In a brutal fight, Jack Bauer wraps a chain around Abu Fayed's neck and hangs him with it, thereby ending the life of a mass murderer and recovering the missing Russian nuclear devices.

11:44pm

President Wayne Palmer announces to the media that Abu Fayed is dead and the nuclear weapons have been recovered. He then becomes ill and collapses, suffering a cerebral hemorrhage and lapsing deep into a coma.

PAYING THE PRICE

Against orders, Jack Bauer brings the Russian circuit board to the Chinese to save Audrey Raines. His plan is botched by CTU—Raines is rescued, but Chinese Official, Cheng Zhi escapes with the damaged component. Cheng asks Phillip Bauer to fix it in return for help to remove Josh Bauer from CTU. The Chinese assault on CTU costs Milo Pressman his life before Bauer ends it and saves Josh. Meanwhile, Vice President Daniels learns that a Russian agent has compromised his lover, Lisa Miller, and the stakes rapidly escalate. To avoid war, Daniels orders Josh Bauer to be turned over to Phillip Bauer in return for the component, but Phillip double-crosses CTU. With Bill Buchanan's help, Jack pursues him to a deserted oil platform, rescues Josh, captures Cheng, and leaves his father to die in a missile strike. The component is destroyed, and war is averted, but Jack's personal torment is not over as James Heller persuades him to walk away from Audrey Raines—Bauer simply has too many enemies to ever protect her. As the day ends, Jack slips away, uncertain where to turn.

12:43am

Moments before being escorted from the premises, Bill Buchanan informs Nadia Yassir in the CTU conference room that he has been fired for political reasons, and she is now in charge.

12:54am

Chinese agents bring a gagged Audrey Raines face-to-face with Jack Bauer for the first time in almost two years—in return for Bauer supplying them with the FB sub-circuit board component.

01:09am

By video conference, Russian President Yuri Suvarov warns Vice President Daniels that a military crisis could ensue if the United States fails to recover the stolen FB sub-circuit board from the Chinese.

01:59am

Former Secretary of Defense James Heller confronts Jack, and warns him to stay away from his daughter. Heller told Bauer "you're cursed, Jack. Everything you touch, one way or another, ends up dead."

FINAL FAREWELL

At 5:55 a.m. on Day 6, Jack Bauer tenderly visits a sleeping Audrey Raines—possibly seeing her for the last time. With great pain, he decides to leave her with her father, realizing he can never protect her from his enemies.

For the first time in many years, Jack Bauer has a reflective moment, but there's no peace in it. As Day 6 ends, Bauer considers all that he has lost through serving the nation, including a chance at happiness with Audrey Raines.

05:59am

| 02:45am | 03:59am | 05:30am | 05:36am |

The Chinese commando leader known as Zhou coldly shoots Milo Pressman dead after invading CTU. Covering for Nadia Yassir, Pressman identified himself as head of CTU, and it cost him his life.

Even though Jack Bauer had just rescued his nephew, Josh, from Chinese agents, Vice President Daniels ordered the boy handed over to Phillip Bauer in exchange for the FB sub-circuit board.

Jack Bauer confronts his father on an isolated oil platform. With a missile strike on the location imminent, Jack abandoned Phillip to his fate. Jack escaped just before the platform exploded.

Having stopped his father, saved his nephew, and captured Cheng Zhi, Jack Bauer went to James Heller's home in an attempt to see Audrey Raines. But Heller convinced him he could never stay with Audrey.

CITIZENS & CTU

Regular civilians often find themselves mixed up in CTU's affairs. Some are sucked in while looking to commit petty crimes or make a big score, some are innocent pawns or helpless victims, some are caught in the wrong place at the wrong time, and some became involved through familial or personal relationships. Following is a list of many of the important civilians who played key roles during the upheavals of Days 1–6.

DAY 1

Frank Allard: Drug dealer, involved with Kim Bauer and Rick Allen. Later set up by undercover cops.

Chris: Friend of Phil Parslow. He tried to help protect Teri Bauer but was killed by a terrorist operative.

George Ferragamo: Keith Palmer's longtime therapist.

Maureen Kingsley: Journalist for *Late Night News* on the CNB News Channel.

Mila Luminovic: Daughter of Nikola Luminovic. She was murdered by Viktor Drazen in her father's restaurant.

Melanie: Rick Allen's girlfriend. She was jealous of Kim Bauer.

Phil Parslow: Doctor. A friend of Teri Bauer, who briefly dated her during her separation from Jack Bauer. He attempted to help her recover her memory, but was killed by terrorists.

Lauren Proctor: Waitress. She was carjacked by and forced to help Jack Bauer as he fled the Santa Clarita Water Plant.

Erica Vasquez: Jamey Farrell's mother. She received money her daughter earned illegally.

Janet York: Kim Bauer's longtime friend from Santa Monica High. She was kidnapped with Kim and murdered by terrorists.

DAY 2

Ralph Burton: A private investigator hired by Kate Warner to investigate Reza Naiyeer.

Frank Davies: A convenience store owner who tried to help Kim Bauer. He was shot and killed by Ramon Garcia.

Danny Dessler: Michelle Dessler's brother. When his affair with Carrie Turner soured, he tried to assault her at CTU.

Al Fulani: Iman of Mosque where Syed Ali prayed. He cooperated with CTU's search for Ali.

Ramon Garcia: A panicked citizen trying to escape nuclear threat. He held up a convenience store for supplies, and was shot by police.

Paul Koplin: Assisted private investigator Ralph Burton in the investigation of Reza Naiyeer. He was tortured and killed by terrorists.

John Mason: George Mason's son. He sold ice cream and was

ordered by his dying father to evacuate Los Angeles with a large sum of money.

Carla Matheson: The wife of Gary Matheson, mother of Megan Matheson, employer of Kim Bauer. She was murdered by her abusive husband.

Megan Matheson: The daughter of Gary and Carla Matheson, cared for and protected by her nanny, Kim Bauer.

Lonnie McRae: Survivalist living in Angeles Crest National Forest. He gave Kim Bauer refuge and briefly held her against her will.

Miguel: A musician and Kim Bauer's boyfriend. He helped her escape Los Angeles and rescue Megan Matheson and was severely injured helping Kim escape.

Reza Naiyeer: Marie Warner's fiancée, a businessman. He was accused of terror activity but was actually a pawn in the terror plot.

Rouse: The leader of a frenzied mob during a nuclear crisis. He assaulted Yusuf Auda and tried to steal money from Kate Warner. He was eventually killed by Jack Bauer while trying to steal crucial evidence.

Cam Strocker: Phone company repairman, taken hostage by terrorists, forced to assist plot to bomb CTU.

Bob Warner: Businessman, CIA informant and the father of Kate and Marie Warner. He was unwittingly used by his daughter, Marie, as part of a terror plot.

Ron Wieland: National Affairs correspondent for a major newspaper, who was detained illegally while investigating reports of a nuclear terror plot.

DAY 3

Luis Annicon: District Attorney who put Ramon Salazar in jail. He was murdered by a prison guard blackmailed by the Salazars.

William Cole: A guest at the Chandler Plaza Hotel. He became infected with the Cordilla Virus, but slipped out of the hotel and came close to starting a major epidemic, presumed dead from the infection.

Danny: A guest at the Chandler Plaza Hotel, who panicked and tried to break out of the hotel after it was quarantined. This forced Michelle Dessler to shoot him dead.

Bruce Foxton: A freelance investigator who helped Wayne Palmer ransack Sherry Palmer's home looking for evidence incriminating her in Alan Milliken's death.

Linda: Kyle Singer's girlfriend, who talked him out of committing suicide.

Ted Packard: The former husband of Dr. Anne Packard. He lost his pharmaceutical company in a drug scandal and later committed suicide.

Craig Phillips: Head of Security at the Chandler Plaza Hotel. He helped quarantine the hotel and was presumed dead from Cordilla Virus infection.

Oriol: The father of Claudia Salazar and Sergio, a farmhand for the Salazars.

Theresa Ortega: Gael Ortega's widow. She murdered Stephen Saunders in a rage while collecting her husband's personal effects at CTU.

Jane Saunders: Daughter of terrorist Stephen Saunders. A college student, she was used by CTU to capture her father.

Sergio: Younger brother of Claudia Salazar, who was under the influence of Hector Salazar. This led his sister to attempt escape from the Salazars.

Douglas Shaye: Ramon Salazar's lawyer, who was murdered by his client.

Helen and Sam Singer: Parents of Kyle Singer who tried to help CTU locate their son.

DAY 4

Nabilla Al-Jamil: Computer science expert. She suspected her boyfriend, Sabir Ardakani, had classified information on his computer and reported it to CTU. She was saved from death by Chloe O'Brian.

Maya Driscoll: Daughter of Erin Driscoll. She suffered from schizophrenia and committed suicide at CTU clinic.

Jason and Kelly Girard: Campers in the desert who stumbled on the nuclear football after discovering Air Force One wreckage. They were chased by Habib Marwan's thugs, and saved by Jack Bauer.

Richard Heller: James Heller's son, and Audrey Raines' brother. He was used by terrorists to help abduct his father.

Naji and Safa: Arab-American brothers, who defended their sporting goods store, with Jack Bauer's help, during anti-Arab riots in the midst of nuclear crisis.

Naseem: Pharmacist, brother of Dina Araz. He did not believe his sister's family was involved in terrorism and was killed by brother-in-law Navi Araz.

Andrew Paige: Computer expert and hacker. This friend and ex-classmate of Chloe O'Brian, discovered an Internet security attack by terrorists and was saved by Jack Bauer.

Debbie Pendleton: Behrooz Araz's girlfriend. She was murdered by his mother, Dina.

Karen Pendleton: Debbie's mother, who searched for her daughter after she disappeared.

Paul Raines: A businessman and Audrey Raines' former husband. His business interests were manipulated by terrorists and he eventually died after saving Jack Bauer's life.

Jen Slater: Tony Almeida's live-in girlfriend while he was out of CTU and drinking heavily.

David Weiss: Attorney from Amnesty Global, who got a court order to save Joe Prado from CTU interrogation.

DAY 5

Cal: Mechanic forced by Ivan Erwich to open Sentox nerve gas canisters, and then murdered by Erwich.

Suzanne Cummings: Walt Cummings' widow. She was comforted by Martha Logan and not informed her husband was a traitor.

Miriam Henderson: Christopher Henderson's wife. She was unaware of his activities and was hurt by Jack Bauer in an effort to make her husband talk.

Derek Huxley: Son of Diane Huxley. He was suspicious of Jack Bauer, and unwittingly followed him to Ontario Airport, where became a terrorist hostage until Jack rescued him.

Diane Huxley: Rented a room to Jack Bauer, whom she knew as Frank Flynn, while he was in hiding. Although she was romantically interested in Bauer, she accepted that he was still in love with Audrey Raines.

Inessa Kovalevsky: Underage girl held as a sex slave by terrorist associate Jacob Rossler, and saved by Jack Bauer.

Barry Landes: Clinical psychologist and older boyfriend of Kim Bauer. They were trapped at CTU during Sentox nerve gas attack, until he took Kim out of Los Angeles at Jack Bauer's request.

Amy Martin: Evelyn Martin's daughter. She was kidnapped by Christopher Henderson as leverage to obtain evidence against Charles Logan from her mother.

Jenny McGill: Lynn McGill's sister, a drug addict. She helped her boyfriend rob Lynn for his CTU keycard, and was murdered by terrorists.

Hans Meyer: Businessman and passenger on the corporate jet taken over by Jack Bauer. He was incorrectly suspected of being Christopher Henderson's courier for the Charles Logan recording.

Carl Mossman: Night shift manager at the bank where Evelyn Martin stored the recording implicating President Logan. He was forced by Jack Bauer to open the bank. He later tried to escape with Bauer and was killed in the ensuing shootout.

Dwayne Thompkins: Drug addict, and Jenny McGill's boyfriend. He stole Lynn McGill's CTU keycard to sell it for drug money, and was killed by terrorists.

DAY 6

Walid Al-Rezani: Head of Islamic-American Alliance, who was forced into a detention center. He reluctantly assisted a sting operation seeking suspected collaborators inside the facility, and was beaten when the operation went wrong.

Marilyn Bauer: Graem Bauer's wife, a former lover of Jack Bauer, and the mother of Josh Bauer.

Josh Bauer: Graem Bauer's son, Jack Bauer's nephew.

Brady Hauser: Autistic brother of Mark Hauser. He was manipulated into using his computer abilities to break through CTU's security protocols.

Mark Hauser: A contractor paid by Dimitri Gredenko to use his brother's computer skills to subvert CTU's security firewall. He cooperated with CTU after being captured by Jack Bauer.

Stuart Pressman: Milo Pressman's brother. He came to CTU to collect his body and personal effects and told Nadia Yassir his brother loved her.

Rita: Darren McCarthy's girlfriend. Seeking to live high on McCarthy's ill-gotten money, she betrayed and killed him. She was murdered by Fayed.

Jillian Wallace: The wife of Ray Wallace. She and her son Scott were held hostage by Ahmed Amar and then saved by CTU.

Ray Wallace: Neighbor of Ahmed Amar. He was forced to help him procure a nuclear weapon component for Abu Fayed after Amar took his family hostage. He was killed in a nuclear explosion.

Scott Wallace: The son of Ray and Jillian Wallace. He tried to befriend Ahmed Amar only to be threatened with death. He was saved by CTU.

Stan: Contractor and neighbor of Ahmed Amar. He was angry at Amar's family and anti Muslim, so he assaulted Ahmed who eventually shot him dead.

INDEX

LONDON, NEW YORK, MUNICH
MELBOURNE, AND DELHI

Senior Editor Lindsay Kent
Senior Designer Nathan Martin
Designers Hanna Ländin & Jon Hall
Brand Manager Robert Perry
Publishing Manager Simon Beecroft
Category Publisher Siobhan Williamson
DTP Designer Santosh Kumar Ganapathula
Production Amy Bennett

First published in Great Britain in 2007 by
Dorling Kindersley Limited,
80 Strand, London WC2R 0RL

2 4 6 8 10 9 7 5 3 1

AD347 – 08/07
24 TM and © 2007 Twentieth Century Fox Film Corporation
24 is produced in association with Real Time Productions
All Rights Reserved

Page design copyright © 2007 Dorling Kindersley Limited

A CIP catalogue record for this book is available from the British Library

ISBN: 978-1-40532-968-2
Colour reproduction by GRB Editrice S.r.l., London
Printed and bound by Hung Hing Offset Printing, China.

Acknowledgements
The author would like to gratefully thank:
Virginia King and Rimma Aranovich of 20th Century Fox for the opportunity and support.

Lindsay Kent, Simon Beecroft, and Nathan Martin of DK Publishing for calm professionalism and support.

Bruce Margolis, Joel Surnow, Jon Cassar, Mariana Galvez, and Alicia Bien

The entire crew behind the making of 24, particularly Joseph Hodges, Rodney Charters, Randy Gunter, Sterling
Rush, Bryce Moore, and Eloy Fernandez; extraordinary prop masters, Hal Lary, Mark Marcum, Claudia Rebar,
John and Chuck Tamburro, and Craig Dyer; special thanks also to photographer, Kelsey McNeal, and his crew.

And most importantly, thanks to the three great loves of my life: Bari, Jake, and Nathan, for temporarily
donating me to this extraordinary project.

Discover more at
www.dk.com